Pockets

skills institute
press

*Distributed By
Fox Chapel Publishing*

FOX CHAPEL
PUBLISHING

A DIRECTORY OF DESIGN DETAILS AND TECHNIQUES

Pockets is an original work, first published in 2011.

Portions of text and art previously published by and reproduced under license with
Direct Holdings Americas Inc.

ISBN 978-1-56523-553-3

Library of Congress Cataloging-in-Publication Data

Pockets. -- First.
    pages cm. -- (Select-n-Stitch Fashion Elements)
Includes index.
ISBN 978-1-56523-553-3
1. Pockets. 2. Sewing. I. Fox Chapel Publishing.
TT560.P63 2011
646.4--dc22
                    2010048405

To learn more about the other great books from Fox Chapel Publishing,
or to find a retailer near you, call toll-free 800-457-9112 or visit us at
www.FoxChapelPublishing.com.

Note to Authors: We are always looking for talented authors to write new books.
Please send a brief letter describing your idea to
Acquisition Editor, 1970 Broad Street, East Petersburg, PA 17520.

Printed in China
First printing: June 2011

Table of Contents

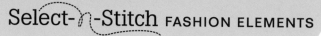
Pockets

Whether you're sewing tailored trousers or a casual jacket, having the right instructions can make a difference in the success of a garment. With step-by-step illustrations and thorough instructions, Select-n-Stitch gives you the in-depth information you need to learn or refine a technique and sew garments successfully the first time.

Use the contents page and Select-n-Stitch guides to find common fashion elements, such as welt or patch pockets, and then flip to the detailed instructions to learn the best methods for constructing them. Whether you're using commercial patterns, modifying patterns, or mixing and matching to make your own creation, use these instructions to complete your sewing projects beautifully.

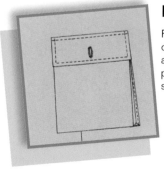

Patch Pockets, page 6

Fun and functional, patch pockets attach to the outside of your garments for easy accessibility and fashion flair. Simple techniques ensure the pieces are properly positioned, flat, and neatly sewn.

Tailored Pockets, page 52

Well-made welt and side pockets are hallmarks of fine tailoring. Learn the best methods to sew common pocket designs so they are smooth and inconspicuous.

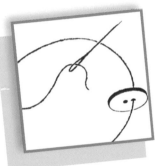

Buttons & Buttonholes, page 134

Buttons are like jewelry for clothes. Learn how to choose, place, size, and sew buttons, and sew strong, attractive buttonholes.

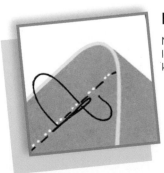

Basic Stitches, page 140

Not sure what an overcast stitch or slip stitch looks like? Find straightforward instructions for key stitches.

Select-n-Stitch Patch Pockets

Fun and functional, patch pockets attach to the outside of your garments for easy accessability. Simple techniques ensure the pieces are properly positioned, flat, and neatly sewn.

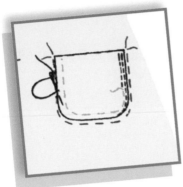

Basic Patch Pocket,
page 8

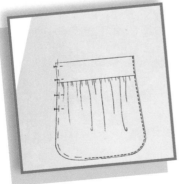

Gathered Pocket,
page 12

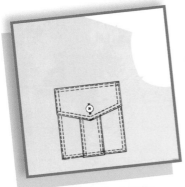

Pleated Patch Pocket,
page 22

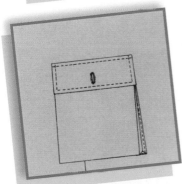

Accordion Pocket,
page 36

Kangaroo Pocket,
page 48

Basic Patch Pocket
Preparing the pocket section

1. Run a basting stitch *(green)* along the pattern markings *(white)* for all the seam lines and the hem fold line.

2. With the pocket section wrong side up, fold down the top hem edge ¼ inch and press.

3. Machine stitch *(blue)* close to the folded hem edge and press again.

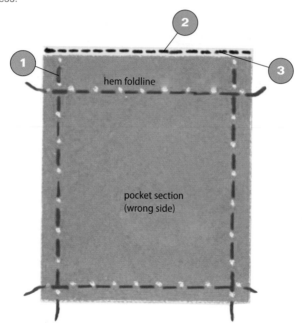

hem foldline

pocket section (wrong side)

Finishing the hem edge

4. Turn the pocket section over, wrong side down. Fold the hem over along the hem fold line and press.

5. Pin and baste *(red)* the hem to the pocket section just outside the basted seam line. Remove the pins.

6. Machine stitch a line along the three seam lines just outside the basted markings. Begin at the folded hem

edge and stitch down to the end of the side seam, then stitch across the bottom of the pocket and up the other side seam to the top folded hem edge. Remove all bastings.

7. Trim the two corners of the hem edge diagonally.

8. Trim both side seam allowances of the hem only to ¼ inch.

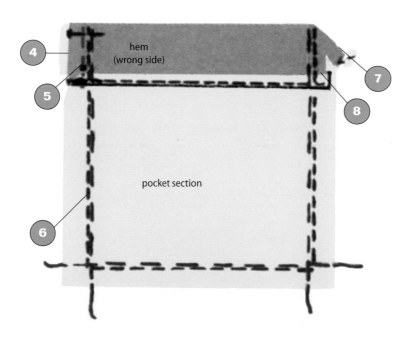

hem
(wrong side)

pocket section

Basic Patch Pocket
Completing the pocket section

Straight pockets

9a. On pockets with straight bottoms, turn the pocket section wrong side up, turn over the hem and press. Then fold in the side seam allowances just beyond the line of machine stitching made in Step 6 and press. Fold up the bottom seam allowance and press.

Pointed pockets

9b. On pockets with pointed bottoms, turn the pocket section wrong side up, turn over the hem and press. Then fold up the two bottom seam allowances that form the point just beyond the line of machine stitching made in Step 6; press. Fold in the side seam allowances and press.

Rounded pockets

9c. On pockets with rounded bottoms, turn the pocket section wrong side up, turn over the hem and press. Notch the curves at ½-inch intervals. Fold in the seam allowances just beyond the machine stitching made in Step 6 and press. Overlap the notched segments where necessary.

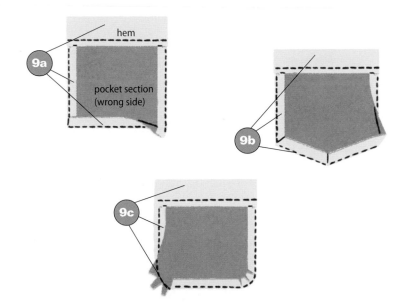

hem

pocket section
(wrong side)

Stitching the pocket to the garment

10. Place the pocket, wrong side down, on the right side of the garment—the side that will be visible when the garment is completed. Align the edges of the pocket with the basted placement lines on the garment that were made when the pattern was cut out.

11. Pin the pocket to the garment at each corner and at 1-inch intervals.

12. Baste along the side and bottom edges of the pocket, ¼ inch in from the edges. Remove the pins.

13. Try on the garment and adjust the position of the pocket if necessary.

Invisible finish

14a. For an invisible finish, hand stitch *(black)* the pocket to the garment with a slip stitch *(page 145)*.

Visible finish

14b. To add strength and give a visible finish, machine stitch the pocket to the garment close to the edge. Add a line of topstitching if desired.

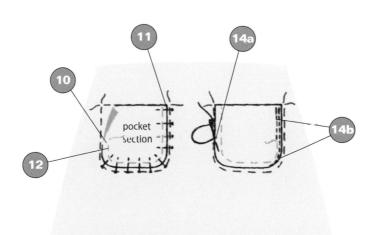

pocket section

Gathered Pocket
Making the pocket pattern

1. To make a paper pattern for a gathered pocket with a band at the top, draw a square the size you want the pocket to be at its widest point. The top of the square will be the top cutting line.

2. Widen the bottom of the pocket by extending the bottom line of the square ¼ inch on each side.

3. Connect the ends of the extended bottom line to the top corners of the square. These diagonal lines will be the side cutting lines.

4. To round the bottom of the pocket, make a dot ¼ inch below the mid-point of the bottom line of the square.

5. Measure up 1 inch from the bottom corner on each of the side cutting lines and make dots at these points.

6. Using a curved ruler or drawing freehand, connect the dot made in Step 5 with each dot made in Step 6 to form a curved bottom cutting line, as shown.

7. To provide fullness for gathers, make three marks across the top cutting line to divide it into four equal segments.

8. Using the marks made in Step 7 as a guide, draw three slash lines to the bottom cutting line. They should be perpendicular to the top cutting line.

9. Cut out the pocket pattern along the cutting lines.

10. Slash into the slash lines up to but not through the bottom edge of the pattern.

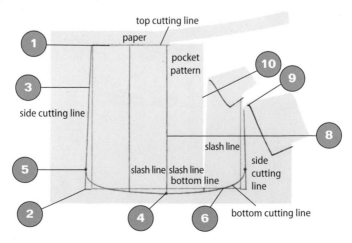

11. Using another piece of paper, draw a vertical line to serve as a guide for centering the pocket pattern. Then center the pattern on the paper.

12. Fan out the pattern by spreading it about 1 to 2 inches apart at each of the slash lines—the sheerer the fabric you plan to use, the wider the spread should be.

13. Tape the pattern in place.

14. Connect the openings in the top edge with smooth lines.

15. Turn the center line into a grain line by drawing in arrow marks.

16. Trim around the pattern outline.

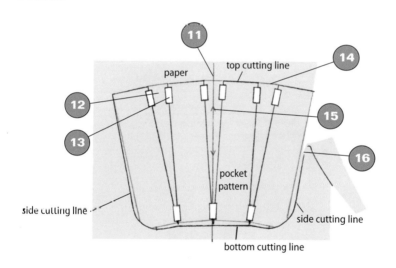

paper
top cutting line
pocket pattern
side cutting line
side cutting line
bottom cutting line

Gathered Pocket
Making the pocket pattern

17. Lay the pocket fabric wrong side up on a flat surface. (To make two pockets, fold the fabric in half lengthwise, wrong sides out.)

18. Place the pocket pattern on the fabric, aligning the grain line of the pattern to the lengthwise grain of the fabric. Pin.

19. Cut along the pattern outline. Remove the pins and set the pattern aside.

20. To cut out the pocket band, draw a rectangle directly onto the fabric with dressmaker's pencil. Make its length the same as the pocket square (*Step 1*) and its width twice as wide as you want the finished band to be plus 1 inch for seam allowances. Be sure to draw the lines with the grains of the fabric.

21. Cut the band along the drawn lines. (If you are making two bands, pin the fabric layers together at the corners inside the rectangle before you cut.)

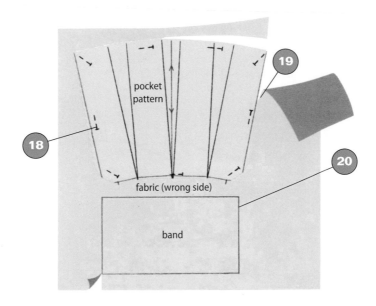

pocket pattern

fabric (wrong side)

band

Attaching the lining to the pocket

22. Cut out from lining fabric a pocket lining for each pocket, repeating Steps 17–19.

23. Trim off ⅛ inch from the side and bottom edges of the lining.

24. Pin together the pocket and lining, wrong sides out, at the top corners.

25. Pull the lining down to the bottom of the pocket and pin the lining and pocket fabric together at the center of the bottom edge.

26. Pin around the bottom and side edges, easing in the pocket fabric evenly between the pins.

27. Baste ³⁄₁₆ inch from the edges. Remove the pins.

28. Machine stitch ¼ inch from the edges, using the presser foot as a guide. Remove the basting.

29. Cut V-shaped notches up to the stitching line at the rounded corners to remove bulk from the seam allowance.

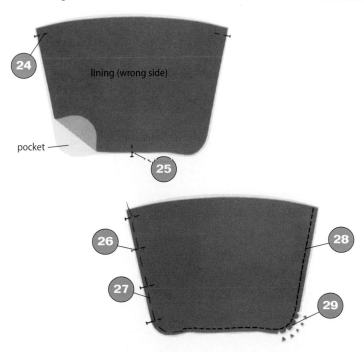

lining (wrong side)

pocket

Gathered Pocket
Gathering the pocket

30. Turn the lined pocket inside out by pushing the bottom up through the unstitched top edge.

31. Roll the stitched edges between your fingers to bring the seam out to the edge. Roll again so that the seam is turned ⅟₁₆ inch onto the lining side and finger-press. Then press with an iron.

32. Set the machine gauge at 6 stitches to the inch. With the pocket lining side down, make two parallel lines of machine basting—one ³⁄₁₆ inch and the other ⁷⁄₁₆ inch from the top edge. Begin and end ½ inch from the side edges. Leave a few inches of loose thread at both ends of the bastings.

33. Turn the pocket so that the lining side is up.

34. Gently pull the loose threads of the bastings on the lining side to gather in the fullness until the top edge is 1 inch less than the dimensions of the square determined in Step 1.

35. Insert pins at each end of the machine bastings and wind the loose threads above and below the pins in a figure 8. Distribute the gathers evenly along the top edge.

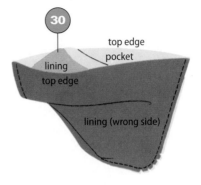

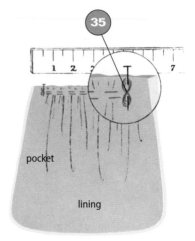

Making and attaching the band

36. Fold the band of the pocket in half lengthwise, wrong sides together, and press in the center crease.

37. Open out the band.

38. Cut a rectangle the same length and one-half the width of the band from an interfacing fabric.

39. Using dressmaker's pencil, draw a seam line ½ inch in from one long edge of the interfacing.

40. Position the interfacing on the band, aligning the unmarked edge with the center crease. Pin.

41. Baste the interfacing to the band inside the seam allowance of the marked edge. Remove the pins from the marked edge.

42. Catch stitch *(page 142)* the interfacing to the band along the center crease. Remove the remaining pins

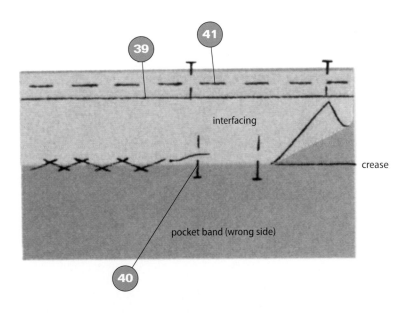

interfacing

crease

pocket band (wrong side)

Gathered Pocket
Making and attaching the band

43. Turn the pocket so that the lining side is down.

44. Center the band on the pocket and align the interfaced edge with the top edge of the pocket. Pin.

45. Baste just above the drawn seam line. Remove the pins.

46. Reset the gauge at 10 to 12 stitches to the inch. Stitch on the seam line across the top edge. Remove the basting and the pins securing the gathers.

47. Trim the seam allowances to ¼ inch.

48. Grade the seam by trimming the seam allowance of the interfacing as closely as possible to the stitching line.

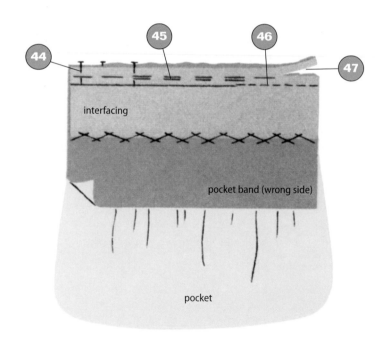

interfacing

pocket band (wrong side)

pocket

49. Turn the band away from the pocket along the top seam. Press the top seam, taking care not to flatten out the gathers.

50. To stitch the sides of the band, first fold down the band along the center crease, then fold up the ½-inch seam allowance on the edge of the band. Pin.

51. Machine stitch ½ inch from each side.

52. Trim the seams to ¼ inch and cut the corners diagonally.

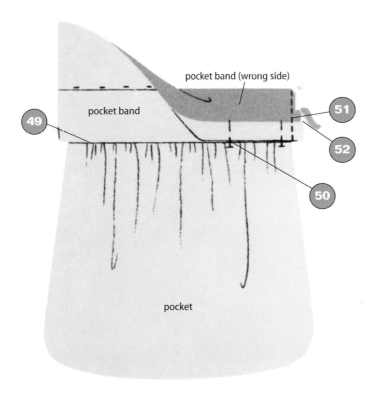

pocket band (wrong side)

pocket band

49

51

52

50

pocket

Gathered Pocket
Making and attaching the band

53. Turn the band inside out through the bottom opening with your fingers, and bring out the corners with a needle.

54. Place the pocket lining side up.

55. Fold under the ½-inch seam allowance on the bottom edge of the band, and press.

56. Slip stitch the band to the lining.

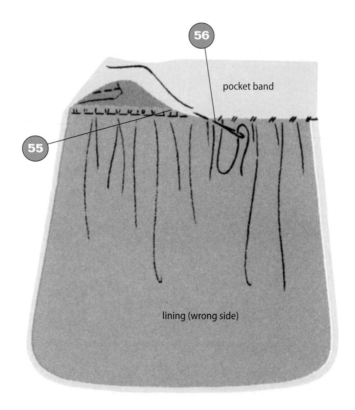

pocket band

lining (wrong side)

Attaching the pocket

57. Pin the pocket to the garment, making sure not to pull the sides out of shape or flatten the gathers.

58. Baste ⅛ inch from the side and bottom edges. Remove the pins.

59. Machine stitch close to the edges. Remove the basting. Press.

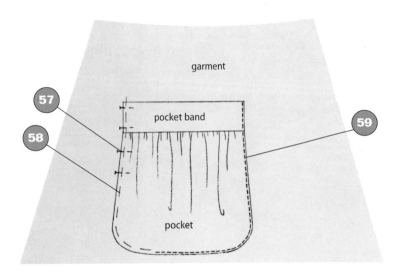

garment

pocket band

pocket

Pleated Patch Pocket
Making the pocket and flap patterns

1. To make the paper pattern for a 4½-inch-square breast pocket, draw a 4½-by-7½-inch rectangle. To make the paper pattern for a 6½-inch-square hip pocket, draw a 6½-by-10½-inch rectangle. The top of this rectangle will be the top fold line of the pocket, the sides and bottom will be seam lines.

2. Draw three cutting lines ½ inch outside of and parallel to the seam lines. Then draw one cutting line 1 inch (1½ inches for a hip pocket) above the top fold line.

3. Extend the top fold lines to the side cutting lines.

4. To mark the pleat, first draw outer pleating lines from the top to the bottom cutting lines 1½ inches (2¼ inches for a hip pocket) in from each side seam line.

5. Divide the area between the outer pleating lines into thirds by drawing inner pleating lines 1½ inches (2¼ inches for a hip pocket) in from each outer pleating line.

6. Cut out the pocket pattern along the cutting lines.

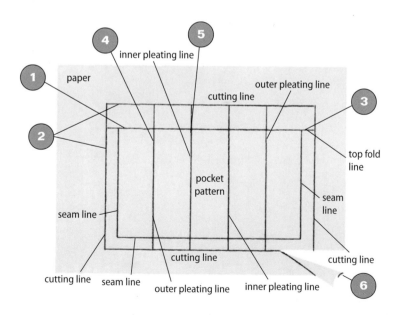

7. To make the paper pattern for the flap, draw the top seam line ¼ inch longer than the finished size of the pocket (*Step 1*).

8. Draw side seam lines from the ends of the top seam line downward and perpendicular to it. Make each line ½ inch long (2 inches for a hip pocket).

9. Mark the bottom of the V-shaped edge midway from the side seams 2 ½ inches (3 for a hip pocket) below the top seam line. Connect this mark with the lower end of each side seam line.

10. For a vertical buttonhole line, measure up from the lowest point of the V-shaped edge a distance equal to the radius of your button plus ¼ inch, and mark. From this mark draw a line equal in length to the diameter of the button plus its thickness.

11. Draw cutting lines ½ inch outside of and parallel to each seam line.

12. Cut out the flap pattern along the cutting lines.

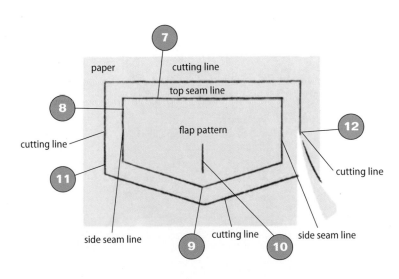

Pleated Patch Pocket

Cutting out and marking the pocket and flap pieces

13. Lay the pocket fabric, wrong side up, on a flat surface. (To make two pockets, fold the fabric in half lengthwise, wrong sides out.)

14. Place the pocket pattern on the fabric, aligning the vertical side edges with the selvage or the lengthwise grain of the fabric. Pin.

15. Place the flap pattern on the fabric next, aligning the vertical side edges with the selvage. Insert pins inside the seam lines so that the lines can be traced onto the fabric without moving the pins.

16. Cut out the patterns. For each pocket, cut out two flap pieces, one to serve as the flap front and the other as the flap facing.

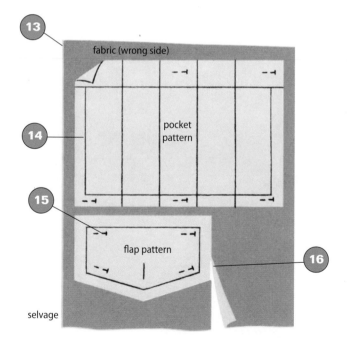

fabric (wrong side)

pocket pattern

flap pattern

selvage

17. To mark the pocket fabric, make a ¼-inch clip into both ends of each pleating line and the top fold line. Remove the pattern.

18. To mark the flap fabric, use a dressmaker's carbon and a tracing wheel to trace all lines—except the buttonhole line—to the wrong side of one of the flap pieces. The marked piece will be the flap front. Remove the pattern.

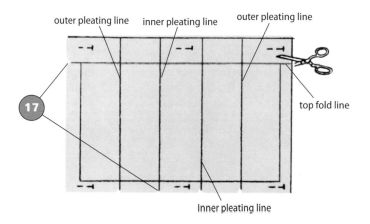

outer pleating line   inner pleating line   outer pleating line

17

top fold line

Inner pleating line

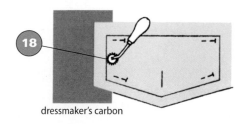

18

dressmaker's carbon

Pleated Patch Pocket
Making the pleat

19. To make a box pleat in the pocket, place the fabric wrong side up.

20. Fold over one side of the pocket at the clip marks for the first inner pleating line and align the top and bottom edges of the fabric. Press in a crease along the fold.

21. Fold the side of the pocket back until the clip marks for the first outer pleating line align with the crease made in the preceding step. Press in a crease along the fold to form the first half of the pleat.

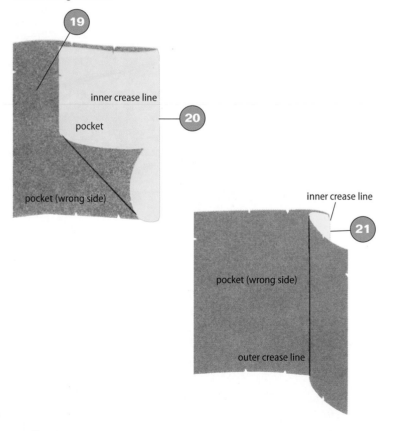

inner crease line

pocket

pocket (wrong side)

inner crease line

pocket (wrong side)

outer crease line

22. To complete the other half of the pleat, turn the pocket 180° and repeat Steps 20 and 21. Make sure the creases of the completed pleat meet exactly at the center of the pocket.

23. To stitch the pleat in place, first flip one side edge of the pocket across the pleat to the other side edge—thus folding the pocket in half with the wrong sides in.

inner crease line

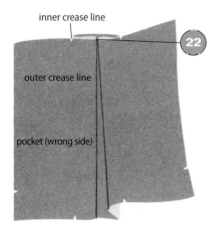

outer crease line

pocket (wrong side)

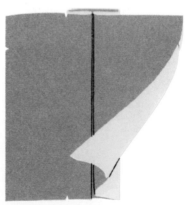

Pleated Patch Pocket
Making the pleat

24. Align the edges and insert two pins near the top of the pleat at the outer creases *(Step 21)*.

25. Starting from the top edge, machine stitch on the outer creases for 2½ inches (3½ inches for a hip pocket), removing the pins as you sew.

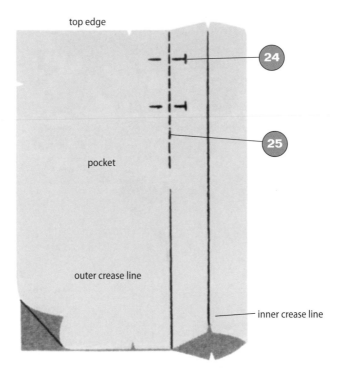

top edge

24

25

pocket

outer crease line

inner crease line

26. To stitch the inner creases of the box pleat *(Step 20)*, first make a row of stitching close to one crease from the top to the bottom edges of the pocket.

27. Make a second row of stitching ¼ inch inside the first row.

28. To stitch the other inner crease, repeat Steps 26 and 27, making sure to push away the rest of the piece from under the edge before you begin.

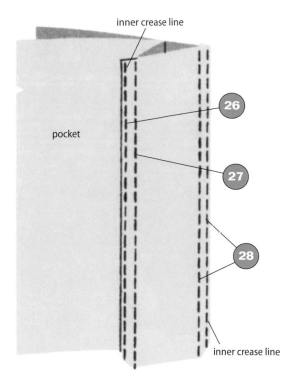

inner crease line

pocket

26

27

28

inner crease line

Pleated Patch Pocket
Finishing the edges of the pocket piece

29. Turn the pleated pocket wrong side up and place it on a flat surface.

30. To make the top hem, turn down the top edge ¼ inch and press in a crease.

31. Turn down the top edge again, aligning the crease with the clip marks that indicate the top fold line of the pocket *(Step 17)*. Press.

32. Baste near the edge of the hem.

33. Stitch along the edge. Remove the basting.

34. Baste the pleats together ⅛ inch from the bottom edge of the pocket.

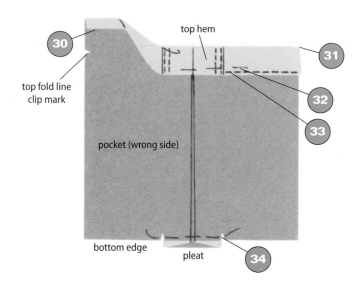

top hem

30

top fold line
clip mark

31

32

33

pocket (wrong side)

bottom edge
pleat

34

35. Turn in each side edge ½ inch and press in the creases.

36. Turn up the bottom edge ½ inch and press in a crease.

37. Unfold the side and bottom edges and trim off ¼ inch of the seam allowances. Then refold the side and bottom edges along the creases.

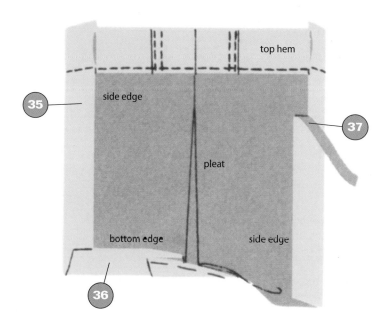

Pleated Patch Pocket
Attaching the pocket

38. Position the pocket on the garment, wrong side down. Pin.

39. Baste ⅛ inch inside the creases along the side and bottom edges of the pocket. Remove the pins.

40. Beginning at one top corner of the pocket, machine stitch close to the edges, pivoting at the corners.

41. When you reach the other top corner, pivot and stitch close to the pocket opening for ¼ inch, then pivot again. Stitch the second row ¼ inch inside the first row of stitching and across the other top edge in the same way. Remove the basting.

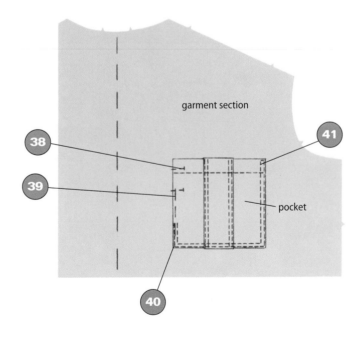

garment section

pocket

Making and attaching the flap

42. Place the flap front and flap facing together, wrong sides out.

43. Ease in the flap front ⅛ inch from the side and bottom edges of the flap facing. Pin.

44. Baste along the side and bottom edges, distributing the ease evenly on the flap front. Remove the pins.

45. Beginning and ending at the top edges of the front flap, machine stitch on the seam lines, pivoting at corners. Remove the basting.

46. Cut the corners diagonally, and trim the seam allowances to ¼ inch. Grade the seam allowances of the facing to ⅛ inch to reduce its bulk.

47. Turn the flap inside out through the unstitched top edge. Pull out the corners with a needle. Press.

48. With the facing side down, make two rows of stitching along the side and bottom edges of the flap following Steps 40 and 41, but in this case omit the stitching across the top corners.

49. Transfer the marking for the buttonhole line from the flap pattern to the front side of the flap. Then make a buttonhole over the marking.

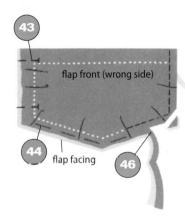

flap front (wrong side)

flap facing

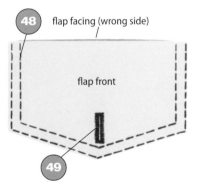

flap facing (wrong side)

flap front

Pleated Patch Pocket
Making and attaching the flap

50. Measure ¼ inch above the top corners of the pocket and make chalk marks on the garment.

51. Place the flap—facing side up—on the garment above the pocket. Position the flap so that the unfinished edge aligns with the chalk marks made in the preceding step, and the side edges align with the sides of the pocket. Pin.

52. Baste ⅜ inch from the unfinished edge of the flap. Remove the pins.

53. Machine stitch across the flap ½ inch from the edge. Remove the basting.

54. Trim the seam allowance to ¼ inch.

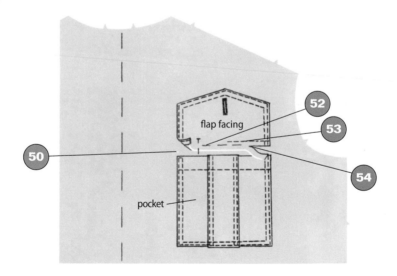

flap facing

pocket

55. Turn the flap down. Press.

56. Slowly machine stitch near the top edge through all the layers of the flap.

57. Make a second row of stitches ¼ inch below the stitching made in the preceding step.

58. Sew the button onto the pocket directly under the buttonhole opening.

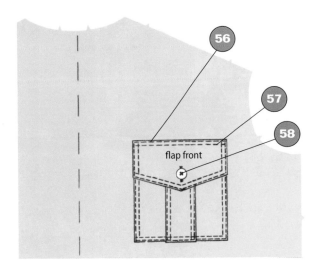

flap front

Accordion Pocket
Making the pattern for the pocket

1. In the center of a piece of paper at least 14 inches square, draw a rectangle that measures 7 inches by 8 inches. Mark one of the shorter lines as the upper edge and the other shorter line as the lower edge.

2. Extend all lines a few inches.

3. To make the pocket wider at the bottom, first measure out ½ inch from the lower corners along the extended lower edge line. Make markings on the line.

4. Connect the markings to the upper corners of the rectangle. Mark these diagonal lines as the side edges.

5. Extend the side edge lines a few inches downward.

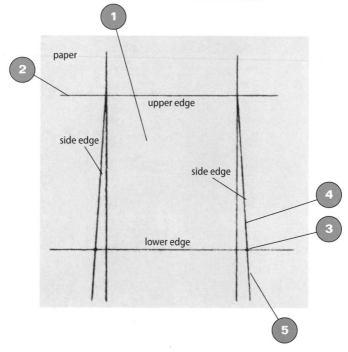

6. To mark accordion folds on the side and the bottom edges, draw two lines 1 inch apart outside of and parallel to each of the three edges, as shown. Mark the inner parallel lines as the inner fold lines, and the outer parallel lines as the cutting lines.

7. To indicate mitered corners, first make markings on each inner fold line 2 inches from the intersections of the fold lines.

8. Next, connect each pair of markings made in the preceding step. Each line should touch its respective lower corner of the pocket.

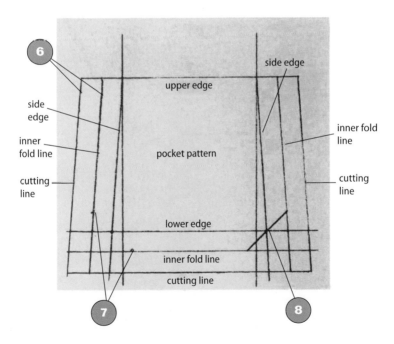

upper edge

side edge

side edge

inner fold line

side edge

inner fold line

cutting line

pocket pattern

cutting line

lower edge

inner fold line

cutting line

Accordion Pocket
Making the pattern for the pocket

9. From each end of the lines made in the preceding step, draw perpendicular lines to the cutting lines. Mark these lines as the seam lines for the mitered corners.

10. To provide the seam allowance, draw parallel lines ¼ inch outside the seam lines. Mark these lines as cutting lines.

11. To mark the hem for the upper edge of the pocket, first draw a line ¾ inch above and parallel to the upper edge line. Make sure the line extends ¼ inch beyond both vertical extension lines.

12. Next draw a vertical line from each end of the line made in the preceding step down to the upper edge line.

13. Cut out the pocket pattern along the outline.

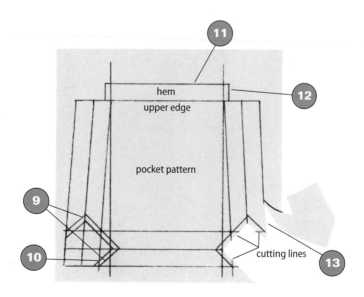

Making the pattern for the pocket flap

14. Place a piece of tracing paper over the top of the pocket pattern as shown, and pin.

15. Trace the upper edge line of the pocket on the paper.

16a. If you want a flap with a straight lower edge measure down 2¾ inches along the side edge lines. Mark.

17a. Draw the straight lower edge of the flap by connecting the markings made in Step 16a. Extend the line ⅛ inch beyond the side edge lines.

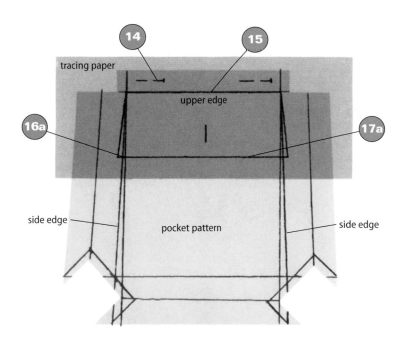

tracing paper

upper edge

side edge   pocket pattern   side edge

Accordion Pocket
Making the pattern for the pocket flap

16b. If you prefer a flap with a curved, V-shaped lower edge, measure down 2½ inches along the side edge lines. Mark. Then mark the lower point of the V midway between the side edge lines and 3½ inches from the upper edge line.

17b. Draw the V-shaped lower edge by connecting the markings made in Step 16b with curved lines. Extend the lines ⅛ inch beyond the side edge lines.

18. Connect the ends of the upper and lower edge lines.

19. To mark a vertical buttonhole line, first measure up from the center of the lower edge a distance equal to the radius of your button, plus ¼ inch. Then draw a line equal in length to the diameter of the button plus its thickness.

20. Remove the tracing paper from the pocket pattern.

21. Draw cutting lines ¼ inch outside of and parallel to each line of the flap.

22. Cut out the flap pattern.

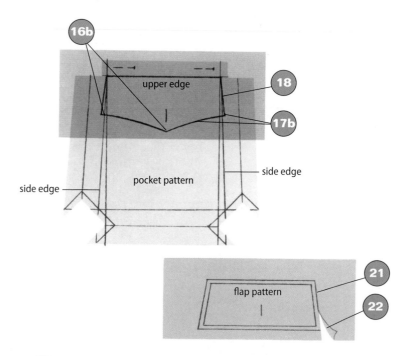

upper edge

pocket pattern

side edge

side edge

flap pattern

Cutting out and marking the pocket and flap pieces

23. Use the pattern pieces to cut out the number of pockets desired. For each pocket, cut out two flap pieces.

24. Transfer to the wrong side of one of the flap pieces all lines—except the buttonhole line. The marked piece will be the front of the finished flap; the unmarked piece will be the facing. Remove the pattern piece.

25. On the wrong side of the pocket piece, transfer the upper, side, lower, inner fold and seam lines. Remove the pattern piece.

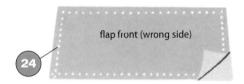

flap front (wrong side)

24

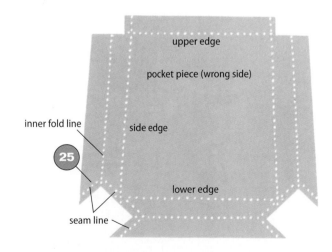

upper edge

pocket piece (wrong side)

inner fold line

side edge

25

lower edge

seam line

Accordion Pocket
Making the mitered corners

26. To make mitered corners, fold the pocket piece, wrong side out, diagonally through one lower corner. Align the edges and markings. Pin.

27. Machine stitch on the lines, removing the pins as you go. Be sure to pivot at the indented corner.

28. Trim the corners diagonally, making sure to remove more of the seam allowance from the bottom corner.

29. Clip into the seam allowance along the inner fold line, cutting up to—but not into—the stitching line.

30. Repeat Steps 26–29 on the other lower corner of the pocket. Press open the seams.

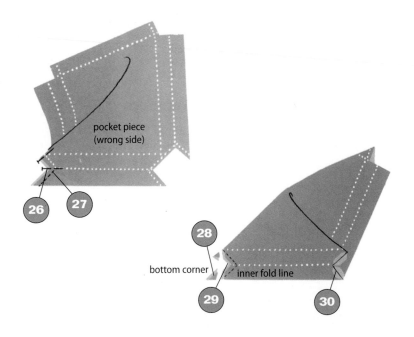

pocket piece
(wrong side)

26 **27**

28

bottom corner inner fold line

29 **30**

Pressing in the accordion folds and the hem

31. Place the pocket piece wrong side up on an ironing board.

32. Fold in along the side and lower edge lines. Press.

33. Fold out along the inner fold lines. Press.

34. Fold in ¼ inch of the raw edges and press. If the lower corners are too bulky to fold in, trim the raw corners as necessary.

35. Fold down ¼ inch of the pocket hem. Press.

36. Fold down again along the upper edge line. Press.

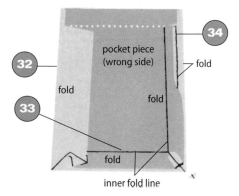

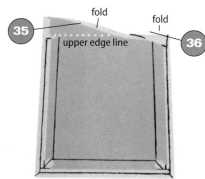

Accordion Pocket
Finishing the hem and attaching the pocket

37. Machine stitch around the edges of the hem, pivoting at the corners.

38. Pin the pocket on the garment.

39. Baste ¾ inch in from the side and the lower edges of the pocket. Remove the pins.

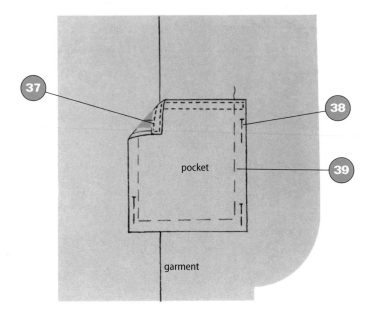

pocket

garment

40. Lift up the first fold of the pocket. Beginning as close to the upper edge as possible, machine stitch along the three sides, pivoting at corners.

41. Attach the upper corners of the pocket to the garment by making a triangular reinforcement at each corner. Stitch first directly over the vertical line of hemstitching made in Step 37. Pivot. Complete the triangle, then stitch again over the first line of stitching. Remove the basting.

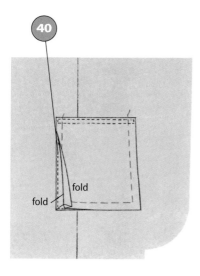

fold

fold

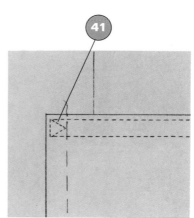

Accordion Pocket
Making and attaching the flap

42. Place the two flap pieces together, wrong sides out.

43. Ease in the top flap piece ⅛ inch from the side and lower edges of the bottom piece. Pin.

44. Baste along the side and lower edges. Make sure to distribute evenly the ease on the top piece. Remove the pins.

45. Trim the seam allowances of the facing so that they are even with the flap front.

46. Machine stitch on the seam lines, pivoting at the corners. Remove the basting.

47. Trim the corners diagonally. Then trim the seam allowance of the facing to reduce bulk.

48. Turn the flap inside out through the unstitched upper edge. Pull out the corners with a needle. Press.

49. Machine stitch ¼ inch inside the side and lower edges, pivoting at the corners.

50. Transfer the marking for the buttonhole line from the flap pattern to the front of the flap. Then make a buttonhole over the marking (page 136).

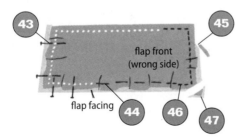

flap front
(wrong side)

flap facing

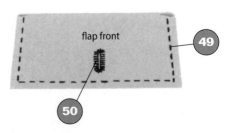

flap front

51. Measure up ½ inch from the top of the pocket and make chalk marks on the garment.

52. Place the flap—facing side up—on the garment, with the unfinished edge toward the pocket. Align the unfinished edge of the flap with the markings made in Step 51. Pin.

53. Baste ⅛ inch from the unfinished edge. Remove the pins.

54. Machine stitch ¼ inch from the edge. Remove the basting.

55. Trim the seam to ⅛ inch.

56. Turn the flap down. Press.

57. Machine stitch ¼ inch from the upper edge of the flap.

58. Sew the button onto the pocket at the position directly under the buttonhole opening.

59. Finish the garment according to your pattern instructions.

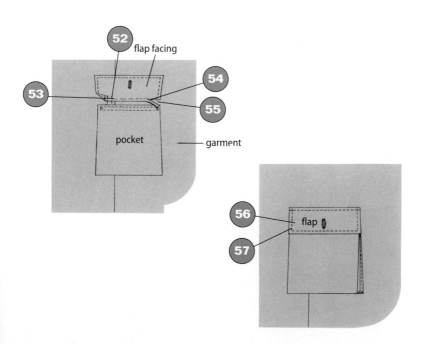

flap facing

pocket

garment

flap

Kangaroo Pocket
Preparing the pocket

1. Lay the pocket piece wrong side up on an ironing board.

2. Turn down the top edge along the seam line; press. Then turn down the side-top edges the same way and press.

3. Fold in one half of the seam allowance of the sides and press.

4. Now fold in the side seam allowances on the seam lines. Press.

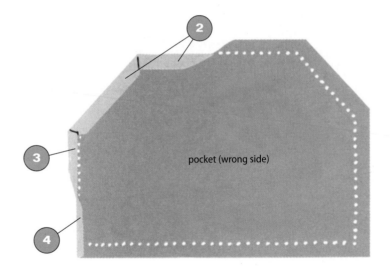

pocket (wrong side)

5. Machine stitch close to the inside edges of the double-folded side seams, beginning ¼ inch below the sloping side-top edges.

6. Make a second row of stitching ¼ inch outside of the first row of stitching, again beginning just below the side-top edges.

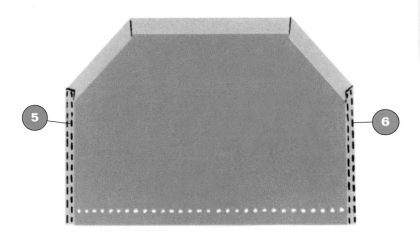

Kangaroo Pocket
Attaching the pocket

7. Position the pocket piece wrong side down in the center of the bodice front, aligning the lower edges. Pin.

8. Baste ½ inch from the edge across the bottom edge of the pocket.

9. Baste the top and the side-top edges ⅛ inch from the edges. Remove the pins.

10. Make two parallel rows of machine stitching on the side-top and the top edges, aligning the rows with the stitchings made on the side edges. Remove the basting from the upper edges only.

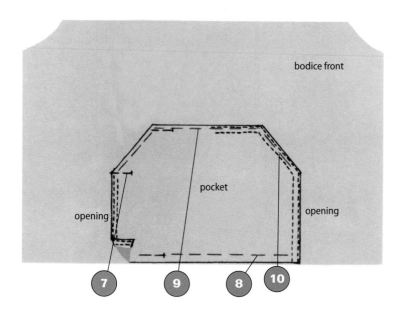

11. Finish the garment, following your pattern instructions.

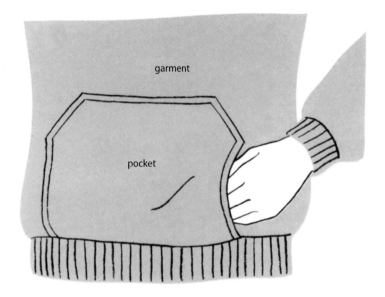

garment

pocket

Select-n-Stitch Tailored Pockets

Well-made welt and inseam pockets are hallmarks of fine tailoring. Learn the best methods to sew common pocket designs so they are smooth and inconspicuous.

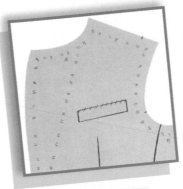

Welt Pocket, page 54

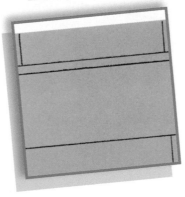

Flap Pocket, page 64

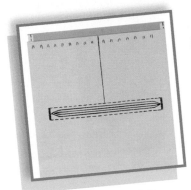

Back Pocket,

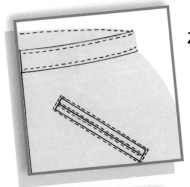

Zippered Pocket,

Side Pocket,

Welt Pocket
Cutting out the welt interfacing

1. Using half the welt pattern, cut a medium-weight interfacing that extends ⅝ inch beyond the pattern fold line.

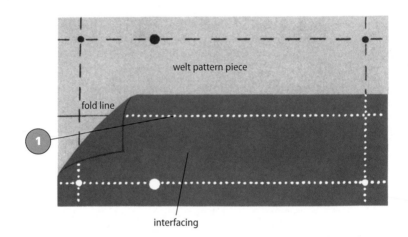

welt pattern piece

fold line

1

interfacing

Attaching the interfacing

2. Cut the welt from the garment material and pin the interfacing to the wrong side of the welt, matching the seam lines and other pattern markings.

3. Baste the left, upper and right edges of the interfacing to the welt just inside the seam lines. Remove the pins.

4. Just outside the fold line, attach the interfacing to the welt with small running stitches, about six to an inch. Use thread the same color as the garment and pick up only a thread of the welt fabric.

5. Trim the seam allowance of the interfacing on the seam line of the three basted sides.

6. Hand stitch the interfacing to the welt along the three basted sides with a catch stitch *(page 142)*, picking up a few threads on the interfacing and then a thread or two on the seam allowances of the welt; no stitches should show on the visible side of the finished welt. Remove the bastings.

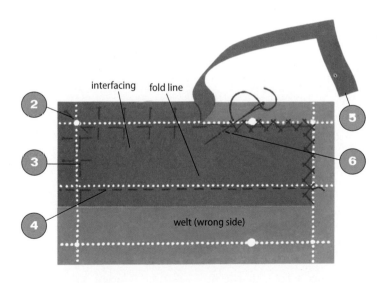

interfacing   fold line

welt (wrong side)

Welt Pocket
Stitching and folding the welt

7. Fold the interfaced welt along the fold line, wrong side out.

8. Pin and baste the folded welt along the seam lines at left and right. Remove the pins.

9. Machine stitch the welt seams at left and right, starting at the fold line and continuing to the upper edge. Remove the bastings.

10. Grade the seam allowances at both ends by trimming the seam allowance on the interfaced half of the welt to ¼ inch and the seam allowance on the noninterfaced half to ⅛ inch.

11. Turn the welt right side out and push the corners out with closed scissors. Press.

12. Baste together the unstitched side of the welt—top in the picture—⅝ inch from the raw edges.

13. Trim the basted edge ¼ inch from the bastings.

14. Apply decorative topstitching or edge stitching if it is called for by your pattern.

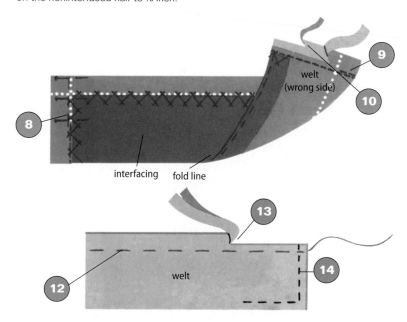

welt (wrong side)

interfacing fold line

welt

Attaching the welt to the garment

15. Unless you have already done so, run lines of basting stitches on the garment along the pattern markings for the stitching lines and the slash line for the pocket opening.

16. Pin the welt to the right side of the garment—the side that will be visible when the garment is finished—matching the basting made in Step 12 to the marking for the lower stitching line.

17. Baste the welt to the garment just below the basting made in Step 12 and remove the pins.

18. Machine stitch the welt to the garment between the two lines of basting. Remove both lines of basting.

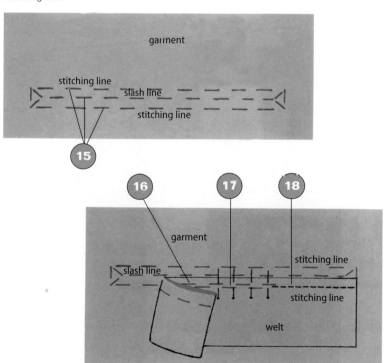

Welt Pocket
Lining the pocket

19. Unless you have already done so, run lines of basting stitches on the pocket lining along the pattern markings for the stitching lines and the slash line for the pocket opening.

20. With the larger part of the pocket lining at the top, place the lining wrong side up on the garment, matching the lower stitching line of the lining to the machine stitching on the welt made in Step 18.

21. Pin the lining to the garment along the basted upper stitching lines and to the welt along the basted lower stitching lines. Be sure to match the ends of the basted markings on lining and garment.

22. Baste along the upper and lower stitching lines, then remove the pins.

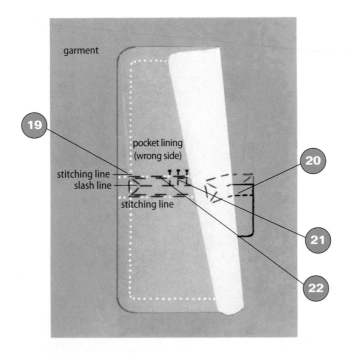

garment

pocket lining (wrong side)

stitching line
slash line
stitching line

23. Machine stitch the upper stitching line through pocket lining and garment; machine stitch the lower stitching line through pocket lining, garment and the two layers of welt fabric. Reinforce both ends of the stitching lines with backstitches. Do not machine stitch along the ends. Remove the bastings.

24. Using small, sharp scissors, cut lining and garment along the basted slash line, first to the apex of the triangular marking at one end and then to the apex of the triangular marking at the other.

25. Carefully clip along the triangle sides toward the ends of the stitching lines, cutting up to—but not into—the machine stitches made in Step 23.

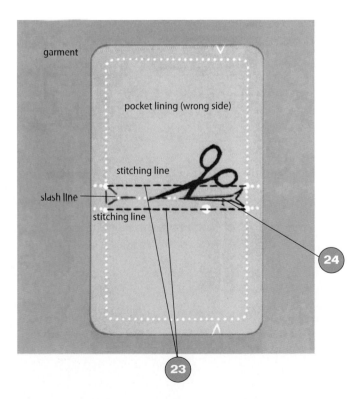

garment

pocket lining (wrong side)

stitching line

slash line

stitching line

24

23

Welt Pocket
Forming the pocket

26. Turn the garment wrong side out and pull the upper and lower sections of the pocket lining through the slash.

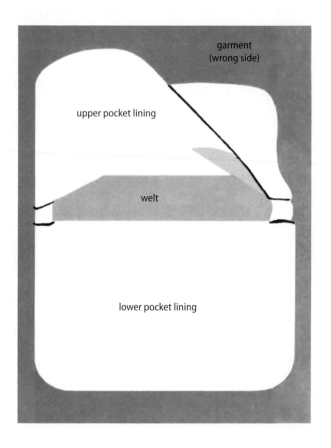

garment
(wrong side)

upper pocket lining

welt

lower pocket lining

27. Flip the upper pocket lining down over the lower pocket lining.

28. Finish the slashed edges of the upper pocket lining and garment fabric with overcast stitches *(page 144)*.

29. Smooth the pocket lining down and press the overcast seam upward.

30. Flip both sections of the pocket lining up and overcast *(page 144)* the seam edges of the lower pocket, welt and garment fabric as in Step 28. Press the seam edges downward.

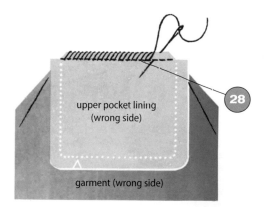

upper pocket lining
(wrong side)

28

garment (wrong side)

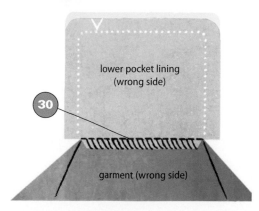

lower pocket lining
(wrong side)

30

garment (wrong side)

Welt Pocket
Finishing the pocket

31. Turn the pocket lining sections down again and pin them together along the sides and bottom, matching seam lines and other pattern markings.

32. Baste, making sure to stitch to the lining the little triangles of lining and garment material formed at each end when you slashed the pocket opening in Step 24. Remove the pins.

33. Push the garment fabric out of the way, so that it lies above and to the left of the pocket lining. Working with the wrong side of the lower pocket lining up, machine stitch along the sides and bottom, being sure to catch the little triangles. Remove all bastings.

34. Trim the seam allowance to ¼ inch.

35. Overcast the raw seam edges as in Step 28.

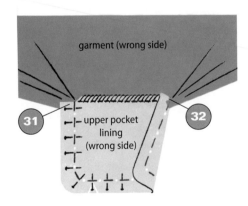

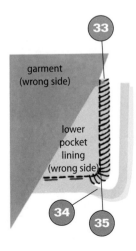

Finishing the welt

36. Turn the garment right side out. Press the welt upward and pin the ends of the welt to the garment. Baste and remove the pins.

37. Slip stitch *(page 145)* the welt ends to the garment, picking up only a thread of the garment fabric close to the welt and sliding the needle through the fold of the welt. Remove the basting and press.

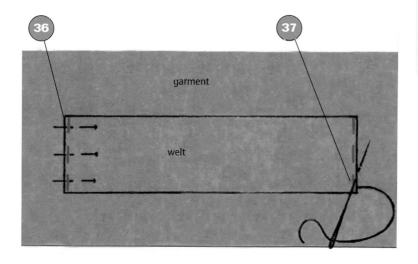

Flap Pocket
Cutting out the pocket pieces

1. Place the jacket fronts wrong sides down on a flat surface. Draw chalk marks to connect the tailor tacks that indicate the position of the pockets. Then baste along the chalk lines.

2. On one of the jacket fronts, measure the distance of the chalk line between the tailor tacks.

3. Measure the distance between the tailor tack marking the front edge of the pocket and the hemline.

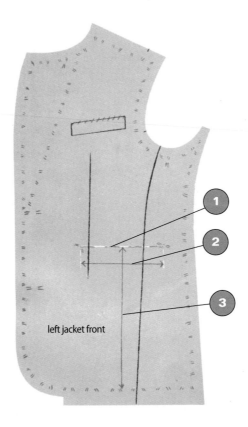

left jacket front

4. Cut out two rectangles from pocketing fabric. The length should be equal to twice the vertical measure determined in Step 3 less 2 inches. The width should be equal to the distance measured in Step 2 plus 2 inches. These pieces will become the pocket bodies.

5. To make the reinforcement patches for the pockets, cut out two more rectangles from pocketing fabric, each patch the same width as the rectangles cut out in Step 4—but only 3 inches deep.

6. Using one reinforcement patch as a pattern, cut out four strips on the straight grain of the garment fabric. These will be the piping above and below the pocket openings. If your fabric is a plaid or a stripe, match the fabric strips to the pattern on the garment at the pocket line.

7. With chalk, indicate with an "X" the wrong side of each strip, and make an arrow showing the direction of the nap, if any.

8. From the jacket lining material, cut out two strips for pocket lining, each strip the same width as the reinforcement patch but 1 inch deeper. Mark the wrong sides with an "X."

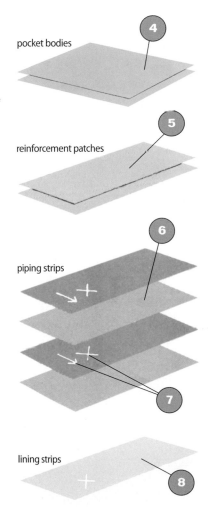

pocket bodies

reinforcement patches

piping strips

lining strips

Flap Pocket
Cutting the flap pieces

9. If your pattern calls for making both sides of the flap from the garment fabric, you will need to revise the pattern before proceeding. To do so, draw ¼-inch seam allowances below the fold line and along each of the sides.

10. Cut along the new seam allowances and discard the bottom part of the pattern piece.

11a. If you are working with a solid-colored fabric, place two pieces of garment fabric together, wrong sides out, on a flat surface.

12a. Pin the revised pattern to both layers of fabric and cut out the flap pieces.

13a. Mark with tailor tacks *(page 146)* the seam lines of both flap pieces. Remove the pattern.

14a. With chalk, mark an "X" on the wrong sides of the pieces.

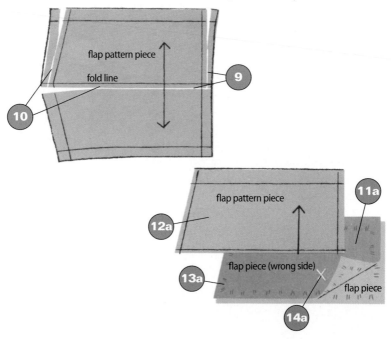

11b. If you are working with a striped or plaid fabric, position the flap pattern on one of the jacket fronts so that the upper seam line on the flap is directly over the chalk line on the jacket. With a pencil, indicate the position of the stripes or plaids.

12b. Place a piece of the garment fabric, wrong side down, on a flat surface. Pin the revised flap pattern to the fabric, matching any stripes or plaid and the direction of the nap—if any. Then cut out the flap piece. Mark the seam lines with tailor tacks *(page 146).* Remove the pattern.

13b. With chalk, mark an "X" on the wrong side of the piece.

14b. Repeat Steps 11b–13b to cut out and mark the second flap piece.

15. Place the two pieces of jacket lining fabric, wrong sides out, on a flat surface. Using the revised flap pattern as a guide, cut out the lining pieces for the flaps. Then mark the wrong sides with an "X."

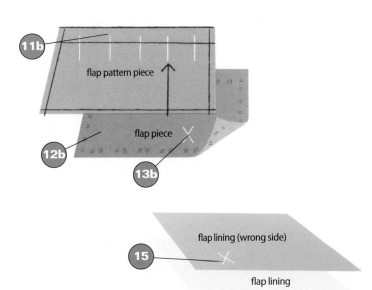

flap pattern piece

flap piece

flap lining (wrong side)

flap lining

Flap Pocket

Assembling the flap

16. Working on one pocket at a time, place the flap lining wrong side down and cover it with the flap piece, wrong side up. Pin the two together.

17. Baste the lining to the flap about ⅜ inch in from the edges. Ease the flap piece in slightly from the edges as you proceed.

18. Machine stitch around the seam lines of the sides and bottom of the flap. At the front corner, curve the line of stitching to produce a slightly rounded corner. Remove the basting and the tailor tacks.

19. Trim the corners close to the machine stitching.

flap lining

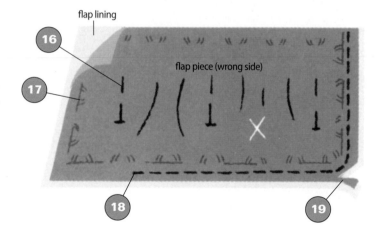

flap piece (wrong side)

Turning and squaring the flap

20. Turn the flap right side out.

20a. Using unknotted thread, insert a needle into the stitching at one corner. Pull the needle through. Then gently tug on the doubled thread to pull out the corners. Repeat until the corner is square.

20b. Square the other corner in the same manner.

20c. To keep the sides straight, baste through all layers ⅛ inch from the three finished welt edges.

20d. Check the size of the welt against the pattern. Then steam press lightly on both sides using a pressing cloth. Remove the basting.

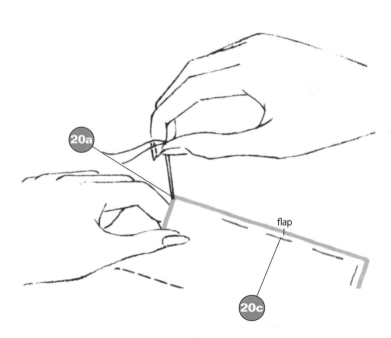

flap

Flap Pocket
Assembling the flap

21. Baste around the finished edges of the flap, rolling the lining back slightly so that the flap fabric is visible around the edges. At the corners, make the basting stitches smaller and tighter so that the flap will curve over the hip when the jacket is worn.

22. Baste the raw edges together at the top, allowing the lining to extend slightly beyond the flap fabric.

23. Repeat Steps 16–22 with the other flap piece and flap lining. Then match the flaps against each other and the pattern. Adjust the shape if necessary.

24. Press the flaps, lining sides up. To preserve the flaps' rounded contours, press one half of a flap at a time, working from the outside edge to the center.

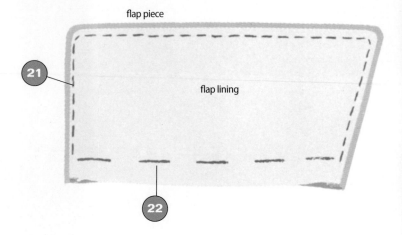

flap piece

flap lining

Lining the pocket

25. Place one of the lining strips wrong side up on a flat surface. Fold up one long side to make a ⅜-inch hem. Then pin, baste, remove the pins and press the hem.

26. Place the lining strip wrong side down over one of the pocket bodies, aligning the unbasted edge of the lining with the pocket edge. Pin. Baste ½ inch from the edge.

27. Baste the folded edge of the lining to the pocket, then machine stitch along the fold. Remove the bastings.

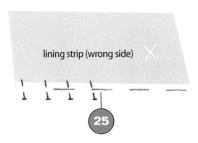

lining strip (wrong side)

25

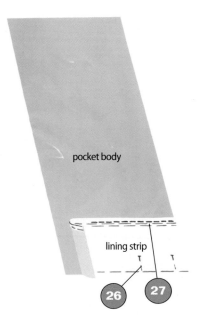

pocket body

lining strip

26 **27**

Flap Pocket
Attaching the piping strips

28. Place one of the jacket fronts wrong side up. Center one of the reinforcement patches, cut in Step 5, over the basted line that indicates the pocket position. Pin. Baste along the upper and lower edges of the patch and remove the pins.

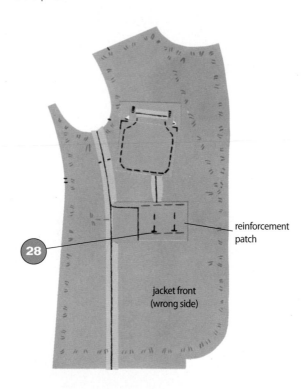

reinforcement patch

jacket front
(wrong side)

29. Turn the jacket wrong side down. Place two of the piping strips—cut in Step 6—wrong side up, above and below the pocket line. The edges of the strips should meet at the line, and the sides of the strips should extend 1 inch beyond the line.

30. Recheck to be sure that any stripes or plaids are matched. At this point, if there is a nap, it should run opposite to that on the garment so that when the piping is finished, the naps will match.

31. Baste the strips to the jacket, ⅜ inch from the pocket line.

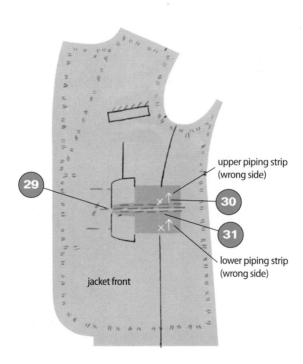

upper piping strip (wrong side)

lower piping strip (wrong side)

jacket front

Flap Pocket

Shaping the piping to the pocket opening

32. Turn the jacket wrong side up. Slash along the pocket line to within ⅜ inch of the ends of the lines of stitching. Cut only the jacket fabric and the reinforcement patch, not the seam allowances of the piping strips on the other side of the jacket. Then cut diagonally up to, but not into, the ends of both lines of stitching.

33. Reach into the slash and pull the lower piping strip through the slash. Then smooth the strip and steam press open the seam allowances.

34. Push the lower piping strip back through the slash.

35. Repeat Steps 33 and 34 to press open the seam allowances of the upper piping strip.

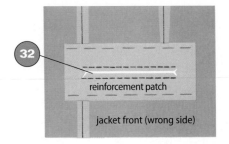

reinforcement patch

jacket front (wrong side)

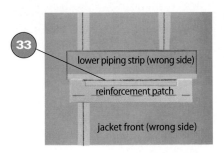

lower piping strip (wrong side)

reinforcement patch

jacket front (wrong side)

36. Turn the jacket front wrong side down. Push one of the piping strips through the slash again, folding the strip over the top seam allowance. This fold will become the piping on the pocket. If the ends of the piping bulge, recheck the diagonal cuts you made in Step 35 to be sure you have cut all the way to the piping stitching lines.

37. Baste through both layers of the piping strip between the fold and the seam, taking care that the piping itself is an even ¼ inch all the way across. (If the fabric is stretchy, make the piping slightly narrower.)

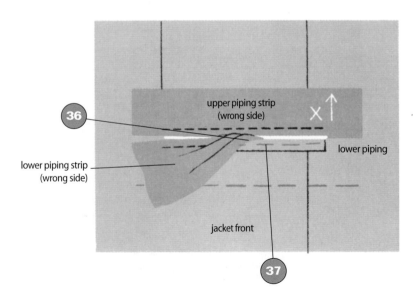

upper piping strip
(wrong side)

36

lower piping

lower piping strip
(wrong side)

jacket front

37

Flap Pocket
Shaping the piping to the pocket opening

38. Repeat Steps 36 and 37 on the other piping strip.

39. Fold up the jacket along the lower piping seam. Turn the lower piping strip away from the jacket, so that the line of stitching on the reinforcement patch is visible.

40. Secure the lower piping strip to the seam allowances with a line of machine stitches, stitching as close as possible to the seam.

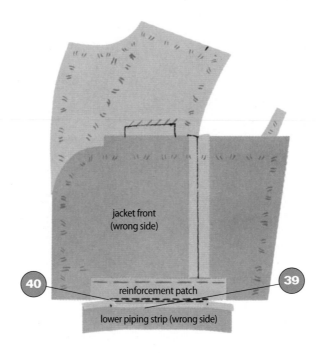

jacket front
(wrong side)

reinforcement patch

lower piping strip (wrong side)

Finishing the piping and the flap

41. Unfold the jacket so that it is wrong side down. Push through the pocket opening the small fabric triangles that were created at each end when you cut the slash.

42. Insert the raw edges of the flap assembly into the pocket opening, so that the top seam line on the flap aligns with the bottom of the upper piping.

43. Pin the flap to the jacket front, checking to see that the flap is straight. The flap should be slightly longer than the pocket opening.

44. Baste along the piping through all the fabric layers, easing the excess flap fabric as you sew so that the flap will curve to the body contour when the jacket is worn. Remove the pins.

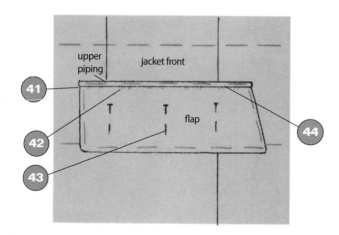

Flap Pocket
Finishing the piping and the flap

45. Fold the jacket front in half, wrong sides out, along the seam of the upper piping, Turn the upper piping strip away from the jacket so that the line of stitching on the reinforcement patch is visible.

46. Secure the upper piping strip and the flap to the seam allowances with

a line of machine stitching, sewing as close to the seam as possible. Remove the basting.

47. Turn the jacket wrong side down and steam press the flap and piping with a pressing cloth, making sure that all the layers underneath are flat.

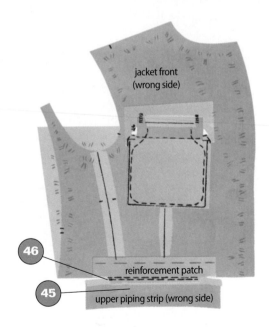

jacket front
(wrong side)

46 reinforcement patch

45 upper piping strip (wrong side)

Making the pocket

48. Turn the jacket wrong side up. Place the pocket assembly, lined side down, over the jacket, aligning the unlined edge of the pocket assembly with the bottom edge of the lower piping.

49. Baste the pocket assembly to the piping ⅜ inch above the edge. Do not catch the reinforcement patch or jacket fabric in the basting.

50. With chalk, draw a seam line ¼ inch from the edge. Then machine stitch the pocket to the piping along the seam line; again, be careful not to catch the reinforcement patch or jacket fabric as you stitch.

51. Turn the pocket assembly over the seam allowances and press the seam flat.

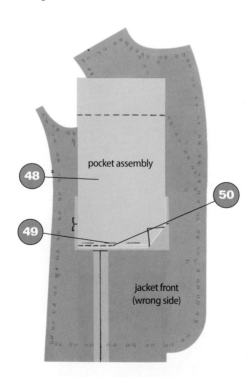

pocket assembly

48

49

50

jacket front
(wrong side)

Flap Pocket
Making the pocket

52. Turn the jacket wrong side down. Fold under both sides of the flap, angling the folds inward. Baste along the sides. Tuck the flap inside the pocket opening.

53. Close up the pocket opening temporarily by making diagonal basting stitches *(page 141)*, catching the upper and lower piping together so that they meet.

54. Turn the jacket wrong side up. Fold up the pocket assembly so that the lined, unattached edge is ½ inch above the seam line for the upper piping. Pin.

55. Baste the unattached edge of the pocket assembly to the flap seam allowance and to the upper piping strip, being careful not to catch the reinforcement patch or the jacket front as you baste. Remove the pins.

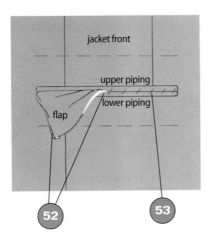

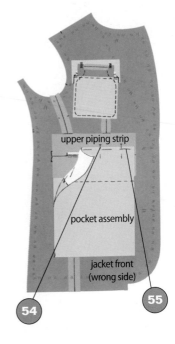

Finishing the flap pocket

56. Fold the jacket front in half, wrong sides out, along the seam for the upper piping. Turn the upper piping strip away from the jacket so that the lines of stitching on the reinforcement patch are visible.

57. Run a line of machine stitching the length of the seam directly over the line of stitching made in Step 49.

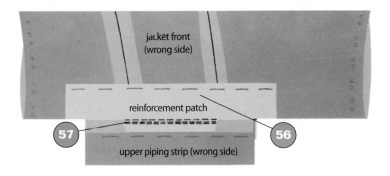

jacket front
(wrong side)

reinforcement patch

57

56

upper piping strip (wrong side)

Flap Pocket
Finishing the flap pocket

58. Turn the jacket wrong side down. Fold back the edge of the pocket opening on one side of the jacket. Smooth flat the pocket and piping.

59. Pull the small, two-layered fabric triangle away from the opening. Then, using the zipper foot on your machine, stitch two or three times across the triangle, reversing the stitching at each end and catching all layers. Stitch parallel with the side seam line, and as close to the pocket as possible.

60. Repeat Steps 58 and 59 on the other end of the pocket opening.

61. Remove the diagonal basting to open the pocket and pull the flap to the outside. Remove the bastings on the sides of the flap.

62. Machine stitch around the sides and bottom of the pocket assembly, starting and ending 1 inch above and ½ inch outside the ends of the pocket opening. Curve the stitches at the corners.

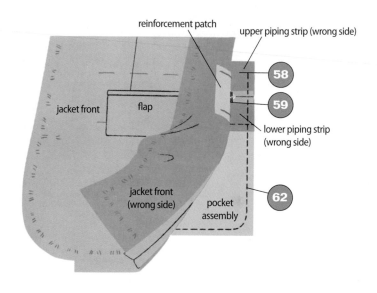

reinforcement patch

upper piping strip (wrong side)

jacket front

flap

58

59

lower piping strip (wrong side)

jacket front (wrong side)

pocket assembly

62

63. With the jacket wrong side down, lift up the flap and sew the lower piping to the flap lining with diagonal basting stitches (*page 141*).

64. Turn down the flap. Using a pressing cloth, press the flap.

65. Finish each end of the pocket opening by making two vertical stitches with buttonhole twist. Make each stitch from the top corner of the upper piping to the bottom corner of the lower piping. End with a fastening stitch on the wrong side of the jacket.

66. Repeat Steps 25–65 to construct the other pocket.

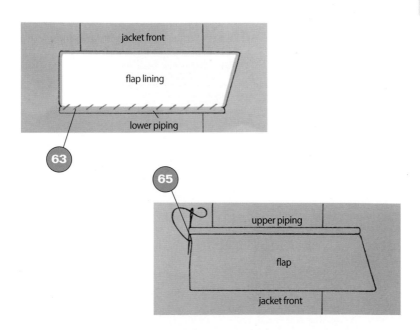

Back Pocket
Determining the position of the pocket

1. Place one of the pants-back pieces wrong side down on a flat surface. Measure the length of the dart seam line. If it is between 3¾ inches and 4 inches long, make a mark at its base with chalk. If the dart is longer or shorter, make the mark 3¾ inches from the raw waistline edge.

2. Make a second mark 2 inches outside the first mark, toward the side seam edge.

3. Align a ruler with the chalk marks made in Steps 1 and 2. Then draw a line for the pocket opening, starting 2 inches from the side edge. To keep the pocket opening in proportion to the overall size of the garment, make the line 4¼ inches long for a 24-inch waist. Increase the length of the line by ⅛ inch for each additional inch of waistline.

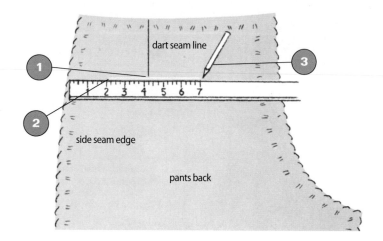

dart seam line

side seam edge

pants back

Preparing the pocket pieces

4. Using a single thickness of pants fabric, cut a pair of pocket piping strips measuring 1½ inches wide and 1 inch longer than the pocket-opening line drawn in Step 3. One long side of each strip should be cut along the selvage edge.

5. In the same manner, cut a pocket facing measuring 2½ inches wide and 1 inch longer than the pocket-opening line drawn in Step 3.

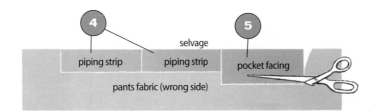

Back Pocket
Preparing the pocket pieces

6. Now cut from pocketing fabric a rectangle 2 inches wider than the pocket opening drawn in Step 3 and—to make the pocket deep enough to hold a wallet—17 inches long.

7. Make a chalk mark ¼ inch in from each side of one short end of the pocketing rectangle. Then make a chalk mark 3½ inches down the long sides of the rectangle and connect the marks.

8. Taper the end of the rectangle by cutting along the lines made in Step 7.

9. Place the pocket piece wrong side down; center a line 1 inch in from, and parallel to, the untapered end. The length of the line should be equal to the length of the pocket opening drawn in Step 3.

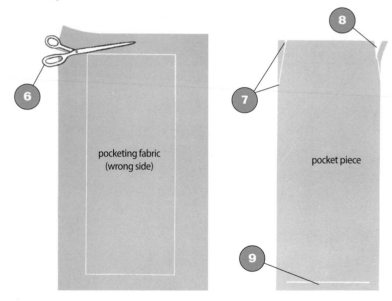

pocketing fabric
(wrong side)

pocket piece

Attaching the piping and pocket piece

10. Lay the pocket piece, wrong side down, on a flat surface, with the untapered end at the top.

11. Position the pants piece, wrong side down, over the pocket piece, aligning the pocket-opening line on the pants piece with the line drawn on the pocket piece in Step 9. Pin the two pieces of fabric together along the line.

12. Baste and remove the pins.

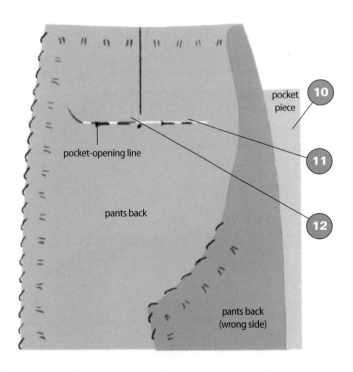

pocket piece

pocket-opening line

pants back

pants back (wrong side)

Back Pocket
Attaching the piping and pocket piece

13. Place a piping strip, wrong side up, just above the basting made in Step 12, with the raw edge of the strip aligned with the stitches. Pin the piping strip in place.

14. On the piping strip, indicate with chalk the ends of the pocket-opening line.

15. Pin the other piping strip, wrong side up, below the row of basting stitches. The raw edges of the two piping strips should meet, concealing the pocket-opening line on the pants back.

16. Baste the piping strips to the pants piece and remove the pins.

17. Beginning and ending at the chalk marks made in Step 14, machine stitch ⅛ inch inside the raw edges of both piping strips, back stitching twice at each end.

18. Remove the basting that marked the pocket-opening line and slash through the pants and pocket pieces along the line. The length of the cut should match the rows of stitching made in Step 17.

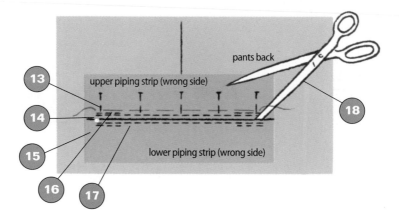

pants back

upper piping strip (wrong side)

lower piping strip (wrong side)

19. Push both piping strips through the slashed opening to the wrong side of the pants piece.

20. Place the pants piece wrong side down. Pinch the top seam of the pocket opening and roll the seam slightly until ⅟₁₆ inch of the piping strip shows below the seam. Pin the piping in place.

21. Repeat Step 20 on the bottom piping.

22. Baste both pipings and remove the pins.

23. Run a line of machine stitches ⅟₁₆ inch below the seam, along the lower piping. Stitch through the pants piece, the pocket piece and the piping strip. To finish the ends of the row of topstitching, leave about 4 inches of loose thread at each end and tie them off on the wrong side of the fabric. Remove the basting from the lower piping.

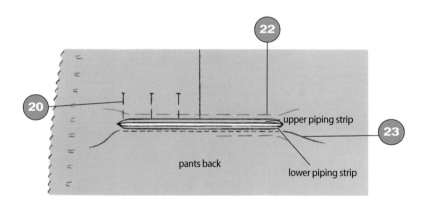

upper piping strip

pants back

lower piping strip

Back Pocket
Attaching the piping and pocket piece

24. Turn the pants piece wrong side up. If the pocketing fabric is a different color from the pants fabric, thread the bobbin of your sewing machine with thread that matches the pocketing.

25. Pull the pocket piece away from the pants back and machine stitch the bottom edge of the lower piping strip to the pocket piece.

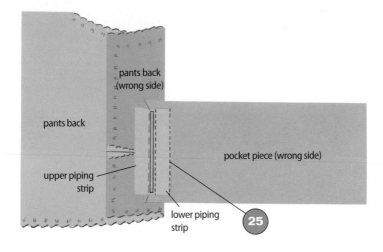

pants back (wrong side)

pants back

pocket piece (wrong side)

upper piping strip

lower piping strip

25

Attaching the back-pocket facing

26. Fold the pocket piece so that its tapered end extends at least ⅝ inch above the waistline edge of the pants. Pin.

27. Turn in the sides of the top layer of pocketing, and make pencil marks on each side at the points that match the upper edge of the bottom layer of pocketing.

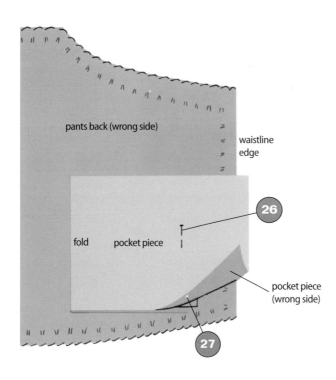

pants back (wrong side)

waistline edge

26

fold   pocket piece

pocket piece (wrong side)

27

Back Pocket
Attaching the back-pocket facing

28. Turn the pants piece so that it is wrong side down, and make a pencil mark on the pocketing fabric at each end of the pocket opening.

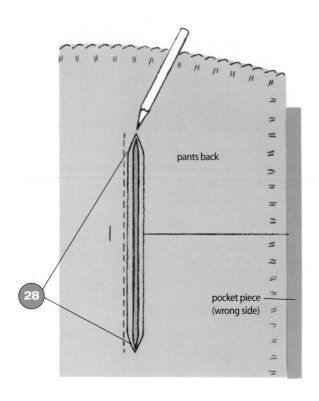

pants back

pocket piece
(wrong side)

28

29. Turn the pants piece wrong side up. Remove the pin holding the folded pocket in place. Unfold the pocket piece and turn it away from the pants.

30. Place the pocket facing made in Step 5 wrong side down on the pocket piece and over the pencil marks made in Step 28. Position the facing so its raw edge extends ½ inch below the marks

toward the tapered end of the pocket, and its ends extend ½ inch beyond the pencil marks on either side. Pin.

31. Baste along both long edges, and remove the pins. Then, using bobbin thread that matches the pocketing fabric, machine stitch ⅛ inch inside the selvage edge of the facing. Remove the basting from the selvage edge.

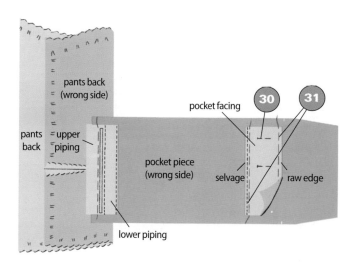

Back Pocket
Finishing the back pocket

32. With the pocket still turned away from the pants, turn the pants piece over, wrong side up, and fold the pocket piece so the pocket facing is up.

33. Turning the side of the pants piece out of the way, match the pencil marks on the edges of the top layer of pocketing to the upper edge of the underneath layer.

34. Pin together the side edges of the pocket piece, then baste and remove the pins.

35. Machine stitch ¼ inch inside the edge of the fabric, and remove the basting.

36. Turn the pocket piece right side out and toward the bottom edge of the pants piece.

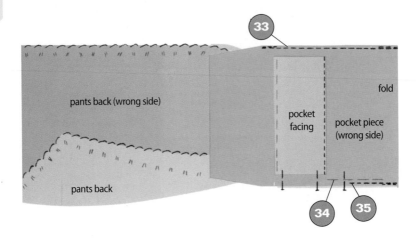

pants back (wrong side)

pants back

fold

pocket facing

pocket piece (wrong side)

37. Turn the pants piece wrong side down, and sew the pipings together with diagonal basting stitches *(page 141)*.

38. Using bobbin thread that matches the pocketing fabric, topstitch ¹⁄₁₆ inch above the upper piping seam, from one end of the pocket opening to the other. Stitch through the pants piece, the piping strip and both layers of pocketing fabric.

39. Machine stitch between the ends of the top and bottom rows of topstitching. Remove all basting from the pipings and from the facing underneath.

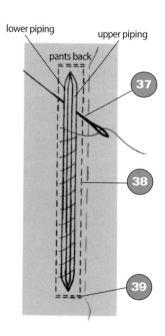

lower piping   upper piping

pants back

37

38

39

Back Pocket
Finishing the back pocket

40. Turn back the outside of the pants to expose the pocket edges.

41. At the tapered end of the pocketing, fold in one raw edge of the pocketing ⅜ inch.

42. Baste from the tapered end to the point where the double layer of pocketing begins.

43. Roll the side seam of the pocket between your fingers so that the seam

is visible. Continue to baste to the bottom edge of the pocket.

44. Repeat Steps 41–43 on the opposite side of the pocket.

45. Rethread your sewing machine with thread that matches the pocketing fabric. Topstitch the pocket ¼ inch inside the fold, starting at one upper edge, continuing across the bottom, and ending at the other upper edge. Remove the basting from the pocket.

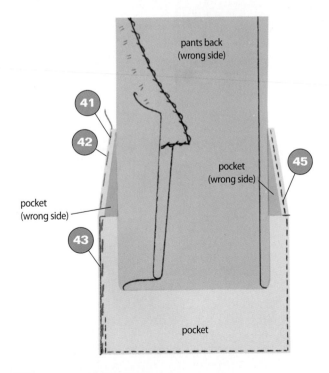

46. Turn the pants-back piece wrong side down, and hand stitch bar tacks *(page 148)* at each end of the topstitching lines.

47. Make a pocket on the other pants-back piece in the same manner.

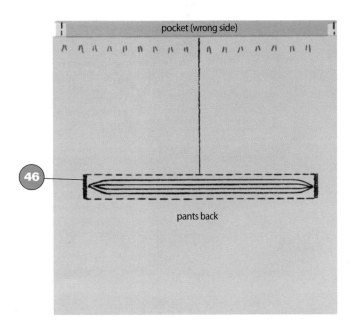

Zippered Pocket
(Demonstrated on a padded/quilted garment)
Preparing the pocket opening

1. Determine how wide you want the pocket to be. The following instructions are based on a 6-inch-wide pocket.

2. With chalk, mark two dots, 6 inches apart, on the garment section where you want the pocket to be. Position the dot that is closer to the center front higher than the other dot, as shown. The angle between the dots should be about 45°.

3. Draw a line—which will be the center line of the pocket—connecting the dots.

4. To mark the outer ends of the pocket opening, draw chalk lines, about 2 inches long, perpendicular to each end of the center line and bisected by it.

5. Complete the opening outline by drawing lines ⅜ inch from and parallel to the center line.

6. Stay stitch just inside the outline, pivoting at corners.

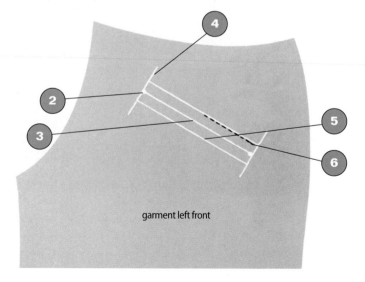

garment left front

Cutting out and making the piping strips

7. Cut from garment fabric two piping strips 2 inches longer than the center line and 1½ inches wide.

8. Cut from nonwoven fusible interfacing two strips that are 1 inch less in length and width than the piping strips.

9. Place the fabric strips wrong side up on an ironing board.

10. Center the interfacing strips, fusing side down, over the piping strips. Press to fuse the strips together following the instructions on the package.

11. Fold the strips in half lengthwise with the interfaced sides together. Press.

12. Set the sewing machine gauge to 8 to 10 stitches to the inch. Then stitch along the folds.

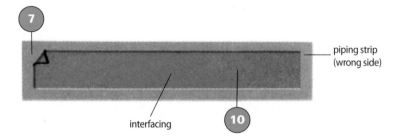

piping strip
(wrong side)

interfacing

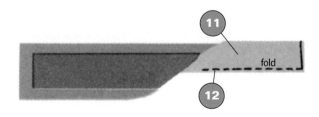

fold

Zippered Pocket
Attaching the piping strips to the zipper

13. Lay face side up a closed zipper 2 to 3 inches longer than the center line. Over it, place one piping strip. Align its stitched side with the center of the zipper, and one short end to the tab end. Pin.

14. Baste, making sure the strip does not shift its position on the zipper. Remove the pins.

15. To attach the other strip on the opposite side of the zipper, repeat Steps 13–14.

16. Turn over the zipper piece.

17. Reset your machine to 10 to 12 stitches to the inch. Then machine stitch on the edges of the zipper tapes. If the zipper tab gets in the way, stop the machine with the needle down; raise the presser foot and move the tab out of the way. Then continue to stitch. Remove the basting.

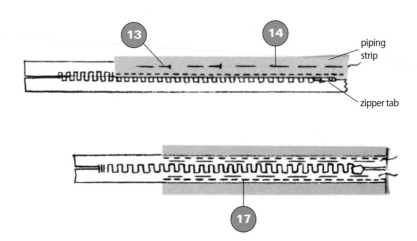

piping strip

zipper tab

Attaching the zipper piece to the garment

18. Position the zipper piece, piping side up, just below the pocket opening markings on the garment. Keep the tab end of the zipper at the lower end of the center line.

19. Pin the bottom corner of the zipper piece to the garment.

20. Without disturbing the position of the zipper piece, slide the tab all the way up, so that the zipper is open.

21. Twist the top half of the zipper piece so that the teeth are turned toward the top of the garment.

22. Align the long raw edge of the piping with the center line. Be certain that the teeth are inside the chalk line that marks the lower end of the center line.

23. Pin the top half of the zipper piece to the garment.

24. Baste along the zipper tape. Remove the pins.

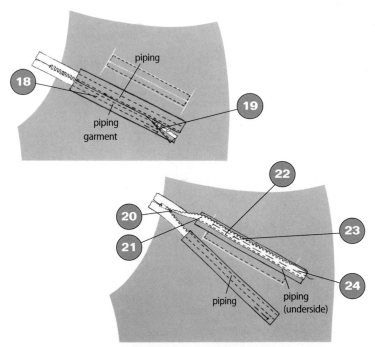

piping

piping
garment

piping

piping
(underside)

Zippered Pocket

Attaching the zipper piece to the garment

25. To attach the other half of the zipper piece, repeat Steps 21–24, but this time twist the piece in the opposite direction, as shown.

26. Machine stitch ⅜ inch from the outside edge of the zipper teeth. This stitching should coincide with the stay stitching made in Step 6. Because of the thickness of the padding, the position of the zipper and garment may slip as you stitch. To check that you are stitching accurately, look at the wrong side to make sure the stitches overlap, then adjust accordingly. Remove the bastings.

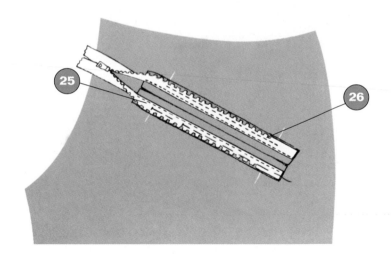

Slashing and preparing the pocket opening

27. Push aside the raw edges of the piping. Then slash the pocket opening along the center line. Start in the middle and slash to within about ½ inch of the ends.

28. Cut diagonally up to, but not into, the stay-stitched corners.

29. Turn the garment wrong side out.

30. Push the zipper piece completely through the opening.

31. Slide the tab all the way down, closing the zipper. Press the seams flat.

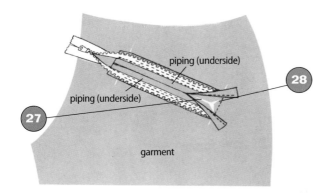

piping (underside)

piping (underside)

garment

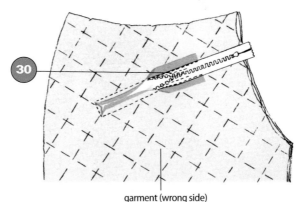

garment (wrong side)

Zippered Pocket
Slashing and preparing the pocket opening

32. Turn the garment wrong side down. Push the loose triangular ends into the side openings.

33. Tuck in the hard-to-reach corners with the tip of a needle. Press, making sure the stay stitching along the side openings is under the crease.

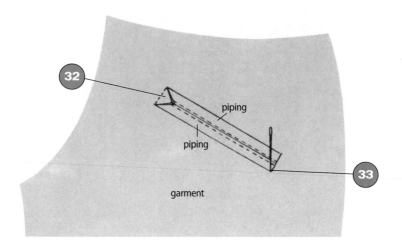

piping

piping

garment

Cutting out and attaching the pocket pieces

34. Cut from a double layer of pocket fabric two rectangles that measure 10 inches in length and 2 inches more than the center line in width.

35. To shape the rectangles, first determine the angle of the slant of the pocket opening, Then mark the angle on one long edge. Connect the mark to the top of the rectangle on the opposite side.

36. Cut through both thicknesses along the line.

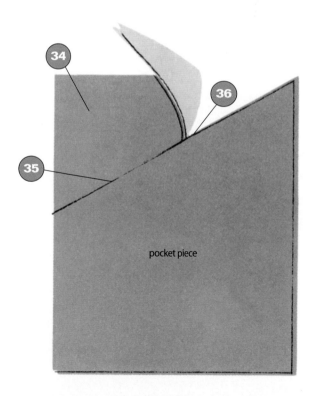

pocket piece

Zippered Pocket
Cutting out and attaching the pocket pieces

37. On the wrong side of the garment, position one of the pocket pieces, wrong side up, over the pocket openings, The slanted side of the pocket piece should be aligned with the bottom edge of the piping below the pocket opening. The longest edge should be toward the top of the garment. Pin.

38. Pin the pocket piece above the opening as shown, to prevent the piece from flopping down.

39. Baste along the slanted edge, Remove the pins, except the one placed in Step 38.

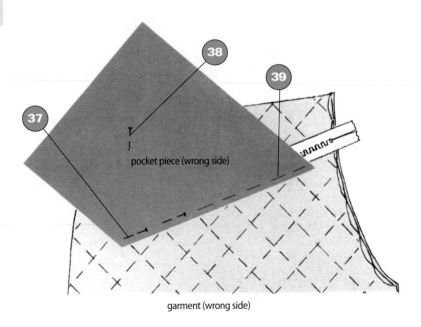

pocket piece (wrong side)

garment (wrong side)

40. Turn the garment wrong side down.

41. Reset the machine to 8 to 10 stitches to the inch. Then stitch along the bottom edge, just outside the piping.

42. Pull the thread ends through to the other side and tie. Remove the basting.

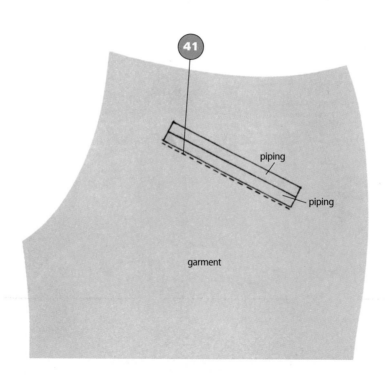

Zippered Pocket
Cutting out and attaching the pocket pieces

43. Unpin the pocket piece and turn it down. Press.

44. Position the remaining pocket piece wrong side up on the pocket opening, so the slanted side is aligned to the top of the pocket opening. The vertical side edges of both pocket pieces should also be aligned.

45. Pin and baste along the top edge. Remove the pins.

46. Trim the bottom pocket piece so that it is the same length as the top piece.

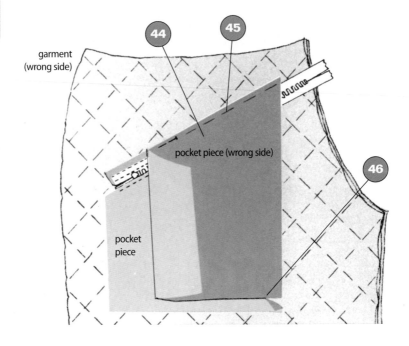

garment
(wrong side)

pocket piece (wrong side)

pocket
piece

Finishing the pocket

47. From the outside of the garment, machine stitch just outside the pipings along the three unstitched sides of the opening, pivoting at the corners. As you stitch the short sides, guide the needle manually by turning the wheel slowly to avoid hitting the zipper teeth underneath.

48. Pull the thread ends through to the other side and tie.

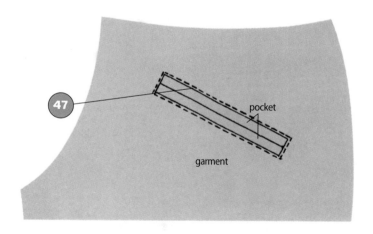

pocket

garment

Zippered Pocket
Finishing the pocket

49. Stitch the two pocket pieces together along the sides and bottom edges, making rounded bottom corners.

50. If the pocket fabric is ravelly and the garment will not be lined, finish the raw edges of the pocket by turning under the seam allowance ¼ inch and stitching. Press.

51. Cut away all but 1 inch of the excess zipper.

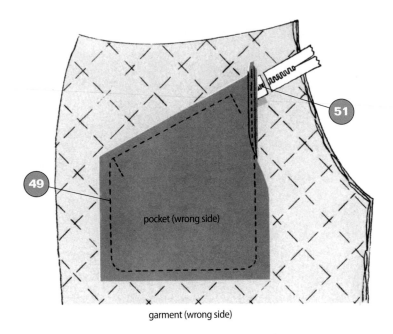

pocket (wrong side)

garment (wrong side)

52. Finish the garment following the pattern instructions.

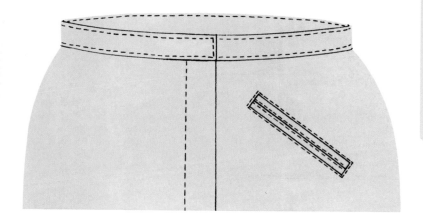

Side Pocket
Preparing the pants pattern pieces

1. If your pattern has the fly piece as an extension of the pants front, cut off the fly piece along the fold line.

2. As a guide for placing the pattern on the fabric, draw a crease line on the pants-front pattern piece. Begin by making a mark along the waist seam line midway between the center-front and the side seam lines.

3. Then, along the hemline, make a mark midway between the stitching lines of the inseam and side seam. Draw a line to connect the two marks.

4. Check the position of the side pockets on both the front and back pattern pieces. Begin by measuring down 2 inches along the side seam lines from the waist cutting line. If the markings for the top of the pocket openings are not located at this point, re-mark them so that they are.

5. Then check the markings for the bottom of the pocket openings. If the pants are to have a waistline 24 inches or less, measure down 5 inches from the top pocket marking. For a larger waistline, add ⅛ inch for each inch of waistline measurement over 24 inches. For example, if the pants will have a 31-inch waistline, measure down 5⅞ inches. Re-mark if necessary.

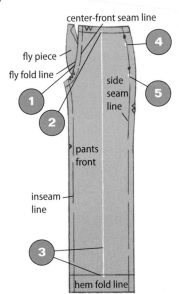

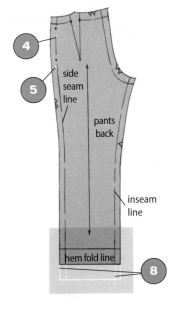

Preparing the pocket pattern pieces

6. Pin together the pattern pieces for the pocket facing and the pocket, matching the seam lines.

7. If the bottoms of your pocket and facing pattern pieces slope toward the inner point, reshape the pattern so that the bottom is straight. This adjustment will keep keys or loose change from falling into the inside corner of the pocket, where they would ultimately fray the pocket. To alter the pattern, first pin the bottoms of the patterns to a piece of tracing paper.

8. Then, draw a horizontal line from the inner pocket point to within 2 inches of the outer edge of the facing.

9. Curve the line, and continue it vertically until it meets the side of the facing pattern.

10. Extend the inner cutting line of the facing pattern onto the corrected bottom part.

11. Trim away the excess tracing paper along the newly drawn bottom line.

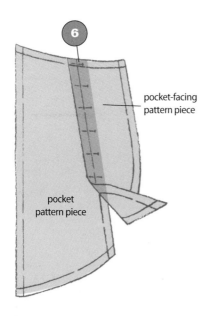

pocket-facing pattern piece

pocket pattern piece

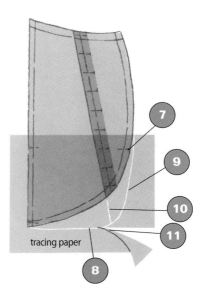

tracing paper

Side Pocket
Preparing the pocket pattern pieces

12. Lay the joined pocket pattern pieces over the pants-front pattern piece so the side seam lines match. The waist stitching line on the pocket-facing pattern piece should align with the waist cutting line on the pants pattern piece. Pin the patterns together.

13. Transfer the corrected pocket-opening markings (*page 112*) from the pants pattern to the side seam edge of the pocket-facing pattern piece.

14. Remove the pins attaching the pants pattern piece to the pocket pattern pieces.

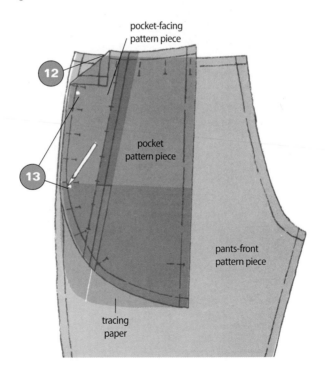

pocket-facing pattern piece

pocket pattern piece

pants-front pattern piece

tracing paper

Cutting and marking the pocket pieces

15. Fold a length of pocketing fabric wrong side out, and lay the joined pocket patterns with the straight cutting edge against the fold. Pin.

16. Cut out the pocket piece.

17. Make a row of tailor tacks *(page 146)* along the stitching line between the newly drawn pocket-opening marks.

18. Repeat Steps 10–12 to make a second pocket.

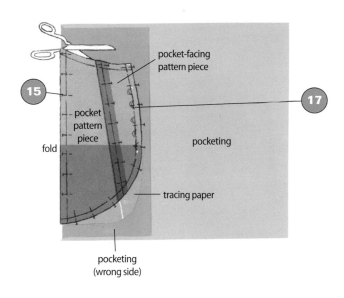

pocket-facing pattern piece

pocket pattern piece

fold

pocketing

tracing paper

pocketing (wrong side)

Side Pocket
Cutting and marking the pocket pieces

19. Open both pocket pieces so that they are flat, and pin them together wrong sides out.

20. Make a mark ⅝ inch below the lowest tailor tack on the left-hand side and ⅝ inch inside the raw side edge of the fabric.

21. Trim the left-hand side of the pocket pieces by cutting first into the pieces at the mark made in Step 15 and then by cutting up along the row of tailor tacks; continue to the top (waistline) edge of the pocket pieces.

22. Separate the pocket pieces and set aside the bottom piece. The top piece will be used to make the left-hand pocket.

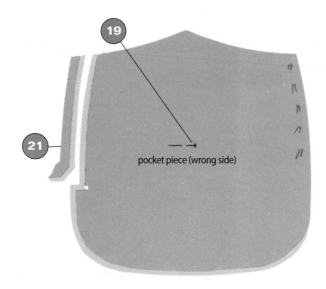

pocket piece (wrong side)

23. Fold the left-hand pocket piece in half wrong sides out, so that the raw edges are aligned.

24. Turn back the raw, unindented edge along the tailor tacks.

25. With chalk, mark ⅝ inch inside the indented edge at the points that correspond with the top and bottom tailor tacks on the unindented edge.

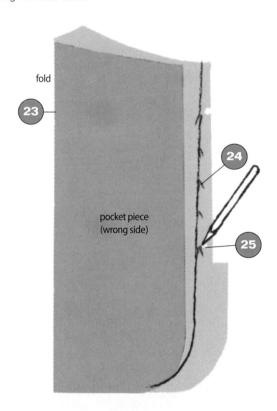

fold

23

24

pocket piece
(wrong side)

25

Side Pocket
Making the pocket

26. Cut a rectangle of paper that is 3 inches wide and 2 inches longer than the pocket opening.

27. Cut the corrected bottoms of the pocket patterns along the extension of the facing cutting line. Separate the pocket-facing pattern piece and its extension from the pocket pattern piece.

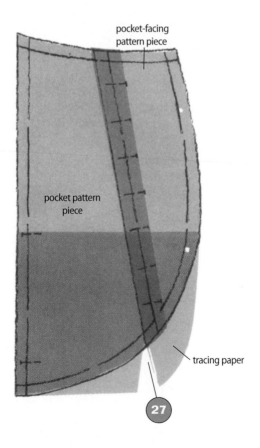

pocket-facing
pattern piece

pocket pattern
piece

tracing paper

27

28. Lay the facing pattern over the paper rectangle. Position the pattern so that the long edge of the paper rectangle parallels the grain line on the pattern. The paper rectangle should extend ½ inch above the top pocket-opening mark on the pattern and 1½ inches below the bottom one. Pin the two together.

29. Trace the contour of the curved edge of the facing onto the paper; then remove the pattern and trim away the excess paper along the drawn line.

30. Using the facing pattern completed in the preceding step, make another facing pattern like the first but 3½ inches wide.

31. Lay the straight edges of the two facing patterns against the selvages of a double thickness of pants fabric, and cut out four pocket facings.

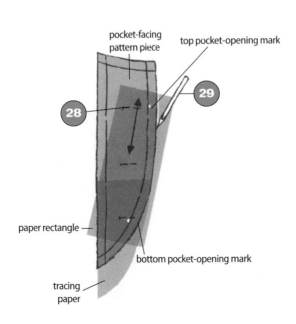

pocket-facing pattern piece

top pocket-opening mark

paper rectangle

bottom pocket-opening mark

tracing paper

Side Pocket
Constructing the pocket

32. Lay the left-hand pocket piece on a flat surface wrong side up, and align the curved edge of one of the narrow facings, wrong side down, along the indented edge of the pocket. The top edge of the facing should be 2 inches below the waistline edge of the pocket piece. Pin the facing in place.

33. Position one of the wide facings, wrong side down, on the unindented edge of the pocket, its curved edge against the row of tailor tacks. The top edge of this facing should be 2 inches below the waistline edge of the pocket piece. Pin the facing in place.

34. Baste both facings to the pocket piece. Remove the pins.

35. Using a bobbin thread that matches the pocketing fabric, start at the edge of the pocket piece 1 inch below the bottom edge of the wide facing, and machine stitch up to the center of the bottom edge. Stitch across to the selvage, up the length of the facing, and continue up and off the waistline edge of the pocket piece. Remove the basting.

36. Repeat Step 35 on the narrow facing.

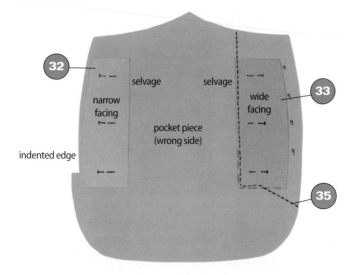

37. Fold the pocket piece in half wrong side out, and align the raw bottom edges of the two layers. Pin. Baste, remove the pins, then machine stitch ¼ inch inside the edge of the fabric from the fold to the bottom of the indentation. Remove the basting.

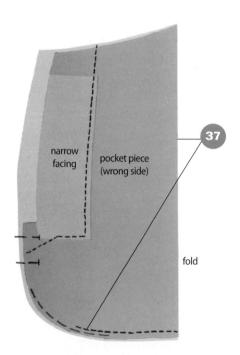

narrow facing

pocket piece (wrong side)

37

fold

Side Pocket
Constructing the pocket

38. Remove the tailor tacks from the unindented edge of the pocket.

39. Turn the pocket over, unindented side up, and fold down the unindented edge to reveal the pocket-opening marks made in Step 25. Pin the turned-down edge out of the way.

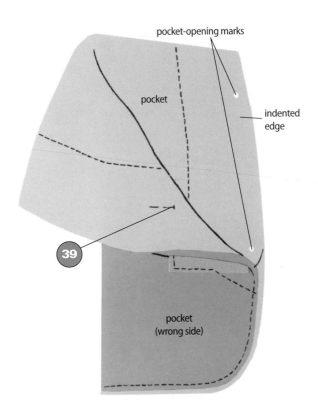

pocket-opening marks

pocket

indented edge

39

pocket
(wrong side)

Attaching the pocket to the pants

40. Lay the pants front, wrong side down, on a flat surface, and place the indented edge of the pocket, facing side down, over it. Be sure to match the pocket-opening marks on the pocket with those on the pants piece.

41. Pin and baste the pants and the pocket together between the marks; then remove the pins, and machine stitch ⅝ inch from the outside edge. Remove the basting.

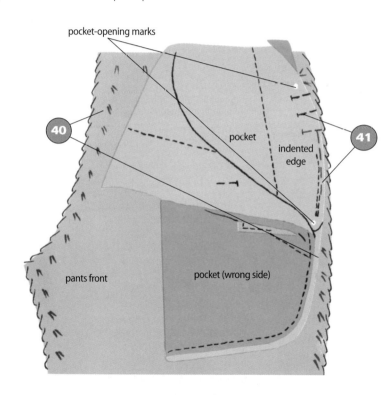

pocket-opening marks

40

pocket

indented edge

41

pants front

pocket (wrong side)

Side Pocket
Attaching the pocket to the pants

42. Make horizontal clips in the seam allowance at the top and bottom of the row of stitching. The clips should come to within ⅛ inch of the stitching line.

43. Trim the seam allowance of the pocket and the facing to ¼ inch between the clips made in Step 42. Do not trim the pants seam allowance.

44. Remove the pin from the top layer of the pocket and fold the pocket to its original position.

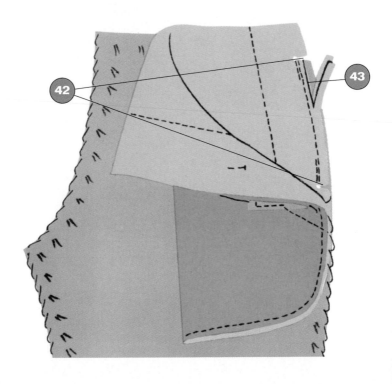

45. Turn the pocket right side out, then turn it to the wrong side of the left pants front.

46. Fold back the top layer of the pocket and pin it out of the way.

47. Roll the seam made in Step 36 between your fingers so that the seam turns slightly toward the inside of the pocket. Pin it in place.

48. Baste, and remove the pins, then machine stitch ¼ inch from the fold. To finish the ends of the row of topstitching, leave about 4 inches of loose thread at the beginning and end of the stitching line.

49. Pull the loose threads to the wrong side of the pocket and tie them off.

50. Remove the pin holding the top layer of the pocket out of the way, and release the wide facing. Repin the pocket out of the way.

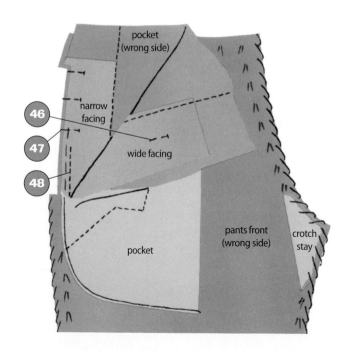

pocket (wrong side)

narrow facing

46

47

wide facing

48

pants front (wrong side)

crotch stay

pocket

Side Pocket
Preparing the side seam

51. Turn the left pants front over, wrong side down, and align the raw side edges with the outer edge of the wide facing. Pin at the top and bottom of the pocket opening.

52. Machine baste over the pins from ¾ inch above the top of the pocket opening to ¾ inch below the top of the pocket opening, keeping the stitching as close as possible to the pocket-opening fold. Repeat at the bottom of the pocket opening. Remove the pins.

53. Make a ⅝-inch-deep horizontal clip through the pants front and the top layer of the pocket at a point even with the top edges of the facings. Fold in the pocket edge above the clip as far as possible, and pin it out of the way.

54. Make a second ⅝-inch-deep horizontal clip on a line even with the base of the indentation in the top layer of pocketing, cutting through the pants front, the top layer of the pocket and both facings.

55. Measure the distance between the clips made in Steps 53 and 54.

56. Cut a rectangle of pocketing fabric 2 inches wide and ¼ inch longer than the measurement made in Step 55. This will be used as a pocket stay to attach the side pocket to the side seam.

57. Place the pocket stay on an ironing board wrong side up, and turn up a ¼-inch hem. Press, then baste the hem.

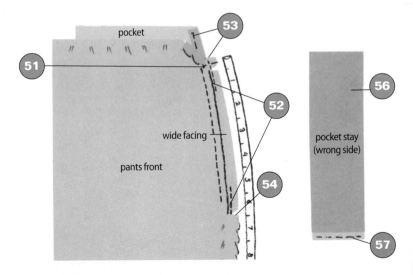

pocket

53

51

52

54

wide facing

pants front

56

pocket stay
(wrong side)

57

Closing the side seam

58. Lay the left pants back on a flat surface wrong side up, and pin the pocket stay, wrong side up, to it, aligning their raw side edges. The upper, unhemmed edge of the stay should be 1¼ inches below the waistline edge of the pants.

59. Baste and remove the pins.

60. Turn the left pants back wrong side down.

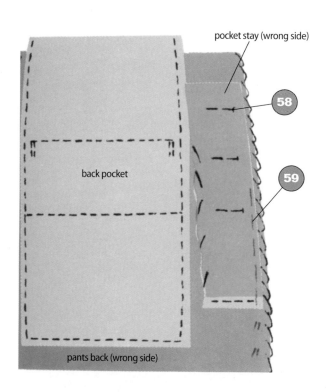

pocket stay (wrong side)

back pocket

pants back (wrong side)

Side Pocket
Closing the side seam

61. Pin the left pants front to it, aligning the side seam edges from the waist to the bottom edge. Baste and remove the pins.

62. Using a zipper foot, machine stitch along the side seam from the waistline edge to 1 inch below the pocket opening.

63. Without breaking the threads, replace the zipper foot with a conventional presser foot, and continue to stitch the side seam to the bottom of the pants leg.

64. Remove the tailor tacks and basting from the side seam and the pocket stay. Remove the machine basting at the top and bottom of the pocket opening. Press open the seam.

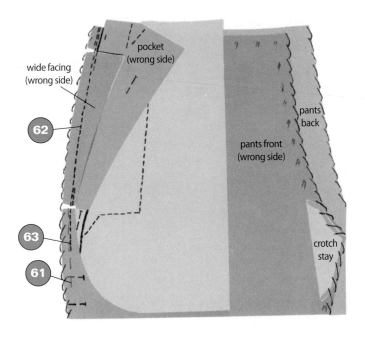

65. At the waistline end of the side seam, tuck the pants-front seam allowance under the side pocket.

66. Tuck the seam allowance below the clip made in Step 54 under the side pocket.

67. Fold the pocket stay over the seam allowance, aligning its raw edge with the seam. Press.

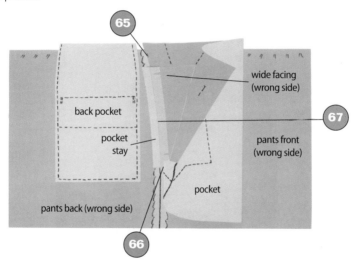

back pocket

pocket stay

pants back (wrong side)

wide facing (wrong side)

pants front (wrong side)

pocket

Side Pocket
Finishing the side pocket

68. Unpin the top layer of the pocket and press flat. Fold the raw edge under so that it extends slightly beyond the fold of the pocket stay. Then pin the folded edge.

69. Baste and remove the pins.

70. Rethread your sewing machine with thread that matches the pocketing fabric, and machine stitch ¼ inch inside the fold from the center fold of the pocket to the waistline edge, rolling the pocket seam slightly under.

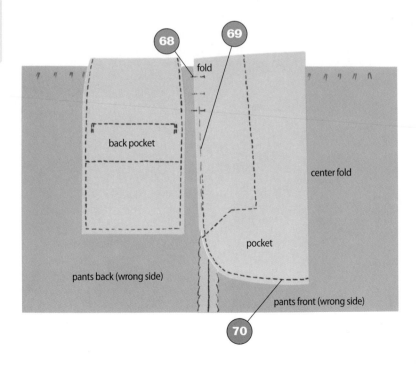

fold

back pocket

center fold

pocket

pants back (wrong side)

pants front (wrong side)

71. Turn the pants wrong side down and sew bar tacks *(page 148)* at the top and bottom of the side pocket between the topstitching and the seam.

72. Unpin the pocket edge pinned in Step 53.

73. Repeat Steps 22–25 and 32–72 to complete the right-hand side pocket.

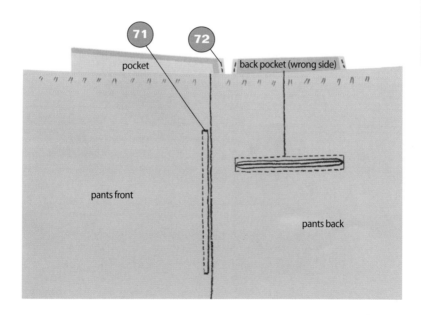

pocket

back pocket (wrong side)

pants front

pants back

Appendix

Whether you're trying a new technique or remembering an old one, sometimes you need more details than the pattern instructions offer. Refresh your basic skills by reviewing useful stitches and sewing procedures.

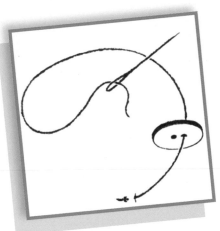

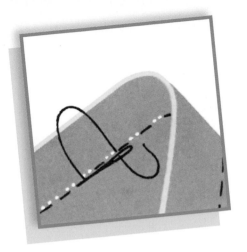

Basic Stitches. 140

Measuring the Button

To find the size of your buttonholes, first measure the buttons to be attached. For a flat, thin button, measure its diameter and add ⅛ inch. For a thicker button, measure its diameter and add ¼ inch. For a mounded or ball button, place a thin strip of paper across the mound or ball, pin it tightly in place, slide the paper off, flatten it, then measure it and add ¼ inch.

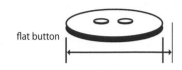

flat button

thicker button

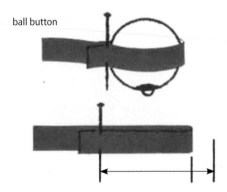

ball button

Buttonhole Stitch

1. Using a knotted thread, insert the needle from the wrong side of the fabric $1/8$ inch down from the top edge.

2. Form a loop with the thread by swinging it around in a circle counterclockwise.

3. Insert the needle from the wrong side of the fabric through the same point at which the needle emerged in Step 1, keeping the looped thread under lhe needle.

4. Draw the thread through, firmly pulling it straight up toward the top edge of the fabric.

5. Repeat Steps 2–4 directly to the left of the first stitch, and continue to make close stitches of even length, forming a firm ridge along the top. End with a fastening stitch *(page 143)* on the wrong side of the fabric.

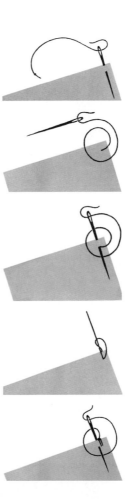

Making the Buttonhole

1a. To make a buttonhole entirely by machine, follow the instructions provided with your particular model.

1b. To make a buttonhole without a special accessory, begin halfway between the placement lines and sew tiny machine stitches ⅟₁₆ inch outside the running stitches that mark the buttonhole position. The stitches should be continuous, pivoting at the corners.

2. With a small pointed scissors, cut the buttonhole along the running stitches, starting in the middle and cutting to each placement line.

3. Sew the buttonhole edges with overcast stitches (page 144), shown in black, to protect them from fraying.

4. Work the overcast edges with a buttonhole stitch (page 135), beginning on the top edge of the buttonhole at the inner placement line.

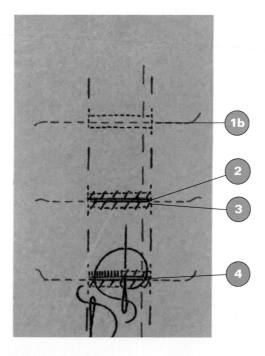

5. At the outer placement line, make five to seven long buttonhole stitches, fanning out about ⅟₁₆ inch beyond the line. Then turn the garment around and repeat for the lower edge. End with a straight vertical stitch at the inner placement line.

6. To finish off the inner edge of the buttonhole with a reinforcement called a bar tack, make three long stitches, side by side, from the top to the bottom edge of the completed rows of buttonhole stitches. These stitches should extend ⅟₁₆ inch beyond the inner placement line.

7. At the bottom edge of the buttonhole, insert the needle horizontally under the three straight stitches made in Step 11, catching the top layer of the fabric underneath. Then pull the needle through, keeping the thread under the needle.

8. Continue to make small stitches across the three long stitches the full depth of the buttonhole.

9. End with two small fastening stitches (*page 143*).

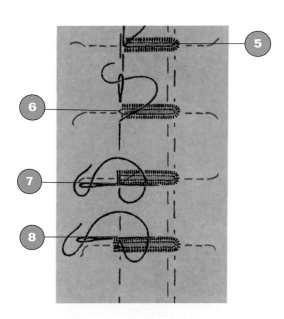

Sewing on Buttons with Holes

1. Using a strand of knotted buttonhole twist, make a small stitch in the fabric at the point where the center of the button is to fall. Insert the needle through one of the holes on the underside of the button and pull the thread through.

2. Hold a wooden kitchen match or a toothpick between the button holes and pull the thread over it as you point the needle down into the other hole. Then make two or three stitches across the match; in the case of a four-hole button, make two rows of parallel stitches across the match.

3. Remove the match and pull the button up, away from the fabric, to the top of the threads.

4. Wind the thread five or six times, tightly, around the loose threads below the button to create a thread shank.

5. End by making a fastening stitch *(page 143)* in the thread shank.

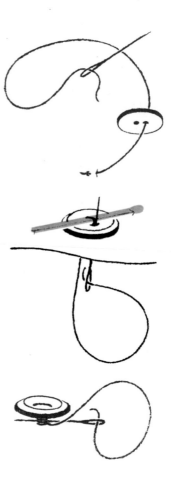

Sewing on Buttons with Shanks

1. Using a strand of knotted buttonhole twist, make a small stitch in the fabric at the point where the center of the button is to fall. Insert the needle through the hole in the shank of the button and pull the thread through.

2. Angle the button away from the fabric with your thumb and take two or three stitches through the button shank.

3. Wind the thread tightly five or six times around the thread shank made in Step 2.

4. End by making a fastening stitch *(page 143)* in the thread shank.

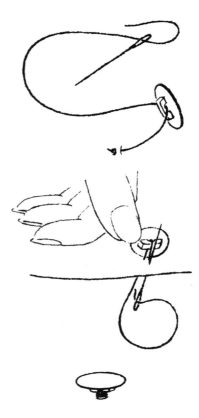

Basting Stitch

Insert the needle, with knotted thread, from the wrong side of the fabric and weave the needle in and out of the fabric several times in ⅛-inch, evenly spaced stitches.

Pull the thread through. Continue across, making several stitches at a time, and end with a fastening stitch. When basting, make longer stitches, evenly spaced.

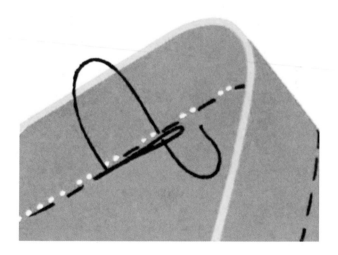

Diagonal Basting Stitch

Anchor the basting with a fastening stitch *(page 143)* through all fabric layers. Keeping the thread to the right of the needle, make a ⅜-inch stitch from right to left, 1 inch directly below the fastening stitch. Continue making diagonal stitches, ending with a backstitch if the basting is to be left in, or a 4-inch-long loose end if the basting is to be removed.

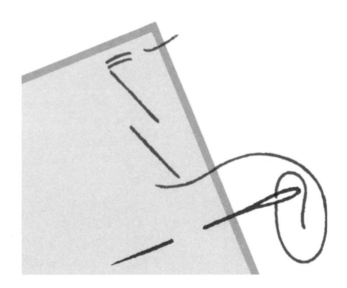

Catch Stitch

Working from left to right, anchor the first stitch with a knot inside the hem ¼ inch down from the edge. Point the needle to the left and pick up one or two threads on the garment directly above the hem, then pull the thread through. Take a small stitch in the hem only (not in the garment), ¼ inch down from the edge and ¼ inch to the right of the previous stitch. End with a fastening stitch.

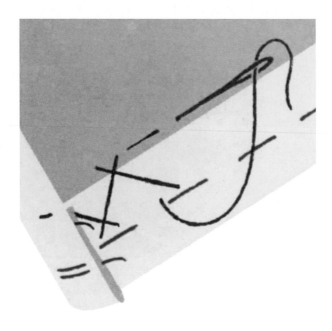

Fastening Stitch

After the last stitch, insert the needle back ¼ inch and bring it out at the point at which the thread last emerged. Make another stitch through these same points for extra firmness. To begin a row with a fastening stitch, leave a 4-inch loose end and make the initial stitch the same way as an ending stitch.

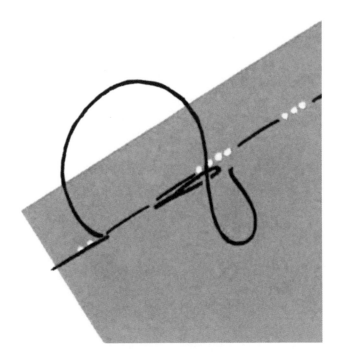

Overcast Stitch

Draw the needle, with knotted thread, through from the wrong side of the fabric ⅛ to ¼ inch down from the top edge. With the thread to the right, insert the needle under the fabric

from the wrong side ⅛ to ¼ inch to the left of the first stitch. Continue to make evenly spaced stitches over the fabric edge and end with a fastening stitch.

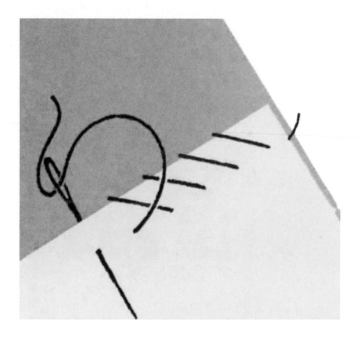

Slip Stitch

Fold under the hem edge and anchor the first stitch with a knot inside the fold. Point the needle to the left. Pick up one or two threads of the garment fabric close to the hem edge, directly below the first stitch, and slide the needle horizontally through the folded edge of the hem ⅛ inch to the left of the previous stitch. End with a fastening stitch.

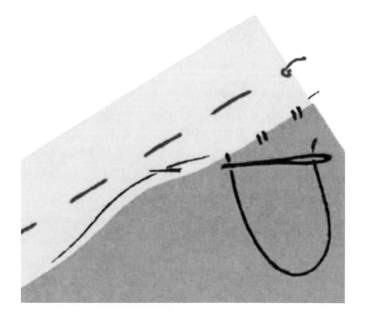

Tailor Tacks

For transferring pattern markings to fabric

1. Using a double strand of unknotted mark-stitching thread, take a ½-inch-long stitch from right to left just outside and at the far right edge of the line to be marked. Adjust the threads so that they are even, then stitch through the paper pattern and both fabric layers.

pants back
pattern piece

2. Pull the threads through, leaving a 2-inch loose end. Then take a 1-inch-long stitch at least ½ inch to the left of the previous stitch. Push the needle all the way through the fabric with the front part of the thimble as shown for two-handed basting, Step 1. Pull the thread through gently, leaving a 2-inch loop on top of the pattern piece. Continue the process, ending the row of tailor tacks with at least 2 inches of loose thread so that the thread does not pull through.

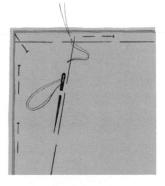

3. If marking only one point, such as the tip of a dart, take a ¼-inch-long stitch, leaving 2-inch-long loose ends. Then take another stitch through the same point and pull the thread through, leaving a 2-inch loop on top of the pattern piece. End with at least 2 inches of loose thread.

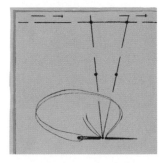

4. Similarly mark all pattern markings. Do not stitch around corners, but after marking one line, begin another at a right angle to the first.

5. Remove all pins and clip through the loops of thread on the top of the pattern. Then separate the pattern piece from the fabric layers. Carefully pull back the top layer of fabric and clip through the exposed threads with the tip of a pair of sharp scissors.

If you are left-handed...
Follow the directions in Steps 1–5, starting at the left edge of the line to be marked and stitching from left to right as shown.

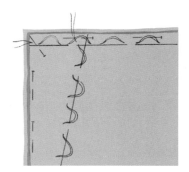

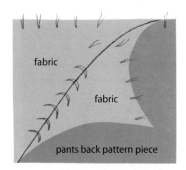

fabric

fabric

pants back pattern piece

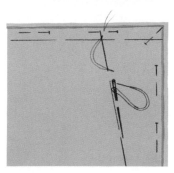

Bar Tacks

To reinforce the ends of pockets or buttonholes

1. To make the thread bar part of the bar tack, use a double thread, or one strand of buttonhole twist, knotted at the end, and bring the needle out from the wrong side of the fabric.

2. Insert it back 1 inch—or however long you want the bar tack to be. Bring out the needle where the thread first emerged.

3. Repeat this fastening stitch two or three times through the same points on the fabric to complete the thread bar.

fabric

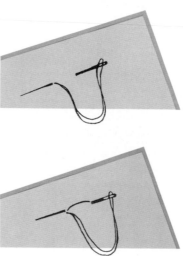

4. Insert the needle under the thread bar at its left edge, and pull it through, tightening the stitch as close to the edge as possible.

5. Continue across the bar, tightening the thread as close to the previous stitch as possible. At the end of the row, insert the needle down to the wrong side of the fabric and secure with a fastening stitch *(page 143)*.

If you are left-handed...
Follow the directions in Steps 1–5, working from right to left as shown.

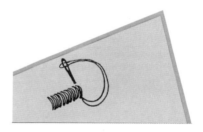

Index

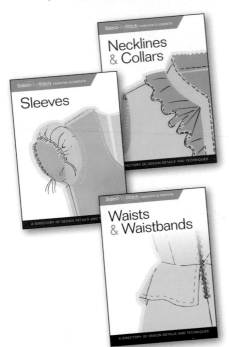